Photographed
Portrait
of an American Home™

100
Home Plan Designs

With Warm Remembrances of the Essence of Home

design basics inc®
HOME PLAN DESIGN SERVICE

Photographed
Portraits
of an American Home™

is published by:

Design Basics, Inc. • 11112 John Galt Blvd.
Omaha, NE 68137

Publisher Dennis Brozak
Associate Publisher Linda Reimer

Editor-in-Chief Bruce Arant
Associate Editors
Priscilla Ivey, Carol Stratman
Managing Editor Paul Foresman
Plans Editor Tina Leyden
Writer Carol Stratman

Art Director Sheri Potter
Graphic Designers
Yen Gutowski, Gloria A. Chavez, Oanh Heiser
Rendering Illustrators
George MacDonald, Silvia Boyd, Shawn Doherty
Research Greg Dodge
Circulation Manager Priscilla Ivey
Technical Advise/Proof Reading
Jody Marker, Cynthia Horan

President Dennis Brozak
Vice President of Operations Linda Reimer

Cover and Title Page Photo: Plan # 1035-PC6
The Barrington Wood, as seen on Page 60.

Builder: Saddlebrook Designers - Builders
Photo By: Jeff Garland

Library of Congress Number: 96-096965
ISBN: 0-9647658-4-5

Table of Contents
100
Photographed Home Plan Designs
Arranged by type in square foot order

Home.

It's a place so familiar, so much a part of you, it's like an old friend. It's where you belong. A place to be proud, to cry, to love and be goofy. The one true place where you feel like yourself – where all that you are practically echoes from its walls. Here, you record your life and reveal yourself to the world. There just may be no greater place on earth.

There are those who will try to tell you that home isn't what it used to be. They'll tell you it's a big mortgage and hiring an interior decorator. But, deep down, you know that's not what it's all about. When you think back, you can clearly recall the more subtle things, that to you, have always made a house a home. The way the kitchen used to smell. The way your bedroom used to feel. You transformed and shaped your home as it, in turn, shaped you. And today, more than anything, you wish for such a place.

Photo courtesy of: Bruce Arant

Photo courtesy of: Lisa Olivo

It's where you want to create memories as pleasantly simple as those of a family taking up a sofa on a Monday night. Indelible times, cuddling with your kids, giving your wife a kiss on the porch or doing the dishes shoulder-to-shoulder with Mom. Your home is your family, those who can make your life so absolutely difficult and yet so completely wonderful. They are forever chiseled into your heart. Your home and your memories of home wouldn't be the same without them.

Home is also graduation parties, birthdays and Thanksgiving cranberry sauce on the table cloth. It's special occasions when relatives come over, pinch our cheeks, and drive us crazy. (Still, we kick ourselves for not inviting them over sooner.) Home becomes a make-shift entertaining place at these times. A familiar place that smells of good food, where we laugh together, watch kids tear into presents and bring up the phrase, "Remember when we..?" It's where everyone is a tad more excited than usual and parents ignore their children's bedtimes to stay just a little longer. We eat too much

and suddenly feel the freedom to sing Irish ballads with Grandma. But who cares? These times make us happy – happy enough to announce, "Christmas is at our house next year!"

But of course, home is yet even more than that. It's where you jumped on your brother's back for many-a-wild and terrifying piggy-back ride. It was a place where you grew up and in your heart where you want your kids to grow up. You remember the front porch, the back yard, and the window seat on a rainy day. It meant playing games like "Red Rover" and "Monopoly" and forever losing to your big brother. There were neighbors and sleepovers and you didn't have a care in the world. You spent your allowance on bubble gum, Batman stickers and a squirt gun. It reminds you of an age and a place you wish you were now and a time you'll never forget.

You want special times to happen there, times like those you remember when certain people touched your life in ways that changed you permanently. These are the people that you think of when "home" comes to mind. They are those who made you laugh, and even now make you smile when you think of them. They were those who took the time for long talks and knew just when you needed a hug. They inspired you to be who you are. You'll never forget them.

We are by and large a culture longing for "home." We know what we want – a home the way we had it. We want a castle that knows us better than we know ourselves. A place that sees our failures and triumphs and keeps us true to ourselves. A place, that when we're there, we're home – we'll just know it. All these dreams, these images of what home really is, are ours at Design Basics. Throughout the following pages, we share some of our finest designs, each created to fulfill your need for a place to call home.

1

Special Places

The home you grew up in was unlike any other to be certain. Modest or extravagant, what made the house so poignant was everything about its whole makeup – its kitchen, basement, porch and living room. Places that became, for you, special places you remember for how they

shaped your life. The bedroom where you sulked after being scolded. The tiny area in the living room between the piano and the wall that was your "perfect place" for Hide and Seek. The spot by the kitchen window where you poured over your homework. And as the home you grew up in shaped your life, so you shaped the home you lived in. There were those wall marks for height, chips in the sink from dropped dishes, or that small dent in the wall from over zealous "rough-housing." "If those walls could talk," we've often said. And if so, they would tell of memories so deeply

engrained in their wood, we'd realize that somewhere along the line, that architectural structure became an undeniable part of us. And we'd realize that home, for all its physical and spiritual meaning, is as much a necessity in our lives as love and oxygen. We'd come to understand that for us, our families, our children – a home is everything.

THE KELSEY

3019-PC6

A Refreshing hybrid:

A quaintly-sized one-story, a deep-set front porch. Double doors walk into a den viewing the front. A rather large kitchen and snack bar. Windows bowed in the breakfast area. And glass shelves in the master bath —a mingling of beauty & function.

Price Code: 14   This home may have been altered from the plan's original design. For more information about the Kelsey refer to the index at the back of the book.

Built by: Helton Homes

Photo by: The Creative Image

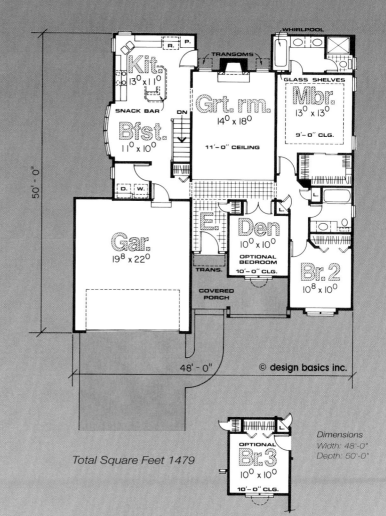

Total Square Feet 1479

Dimensions
Width: 48'-0"
Depth: 50'-0"

Dimensions
Width: 60'-0"
Depth: 58'-0"

Total	2645 Sq. Ft.
Main	1972 Sq. Ft.
Second	673 Sq. Ft.

THE ARMBURST

2723-PC6

An air of vivid pleasantry in the marriage of brick and stucco.

Double doors to a den with spider-beamed ceiling. See-through fireplace between
"at-home" living areas. Wide laundry room. The usual amenities of greatness in the
master bath: an oval whirlpool tub. Shower with seat. His and her vanitites.

Price Code: 26

This home may have been altered from the plan's original design. For more information
on the Armburst refer to the index at the back of the book.

*Top Left: From the entry, a welcome into the
great room with three arched windows.*

*Below Left: A decorative ceiling and French
doors open to a luxurious bath–
all in the master suite.*

*Below Center: His and her vanities and a
whirlpool tub pampering the master bath.*

Built by: Douglas Young Builder

Photos by: Tom Weigand

THE LANCASTER

1752-PC6

A shady porch wrapped in luxuriant foliage.

Windows —lining the rear of the great room, breakfast area and kitchen. Light given to spaciousness. His and her walk-in closets in the master bedroom. A view out the front and below from the upstairs landing. More light. More spaciousness.

Price Code: 18   This home may have been altered from the plan's original design. For more information about the Lancaster refer to the index at the back of the book.

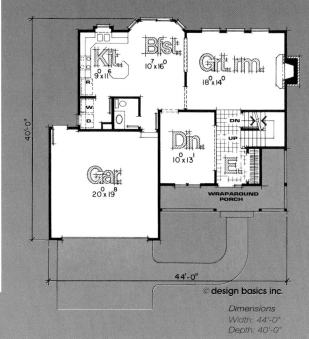

© design basics inc.

Dimensions
Width: 44'-0"
Depth: 40'-0"

Total	1846 Sq. Ft.
Main	919 Sq. Ft.
Second	927 Sq. Ft.

ALL PLANS Customizable

Built by: J.F. Duggan Construction

THE BANCROFT

1559-PC6

A thick stripe of clouds. A front porch. A day for indulging oneself.

For the casual party, a long snack bar, see-through fireplace, wet bar —all within the great room and kitchen. Freezer space in the laundry room. And storage in the garage. A sloped ceiling and boxed windows drawing attention to the master bath.

Price Code: 18   This home may have been altered from the plan's original design. For more information about the Bancroft refer to the index at the back of the book.

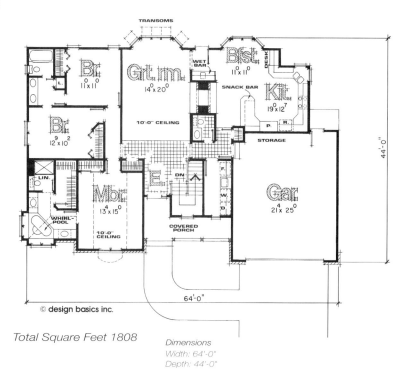

© design basics inc.

Total Square Feet 1808

Dimensions
Width: 64'-0"
Depth: 44'-0"

A setting sun. Cool clouds resting above a stone and stucco variation.

Through a set of double doors, a private master suite and down the hall its own den.

A fireplace, wet bar and entertainment center — enjoyment from either the great room or hearth room/kitche

Price Code: 25

This home may have been altered from the plan's original design. For more information about the Edmonton refer to the index at the back of the book.

THE EDMONTON

2309-PC6

Top Left: The island kitchen with the convenience of a walk-in pantry.

Middle Left: A perspective into the hearth room with changes to the entertainment center.

Middle Right: A view of the the entry from the stylish great room.

Far Right: Modifications in the master suite- The double vanity viewed through an arched opening instead of a door.

Built by: Classic Custom Builders

Photos by: The Image Engineer

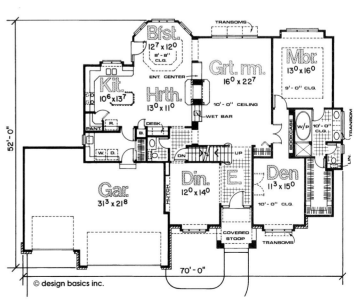

Total	2579 Sq. Ft.
Main	1933 Sq. Ft.
Second	646 Sq. Ft.

Dimensions
Width: 70'-0"
Depth: 52'-0"

ALL PLANS *Customizable*

© design basics inc.

THE EDMONTON 2309-PC6

Above: Statuesque columns frame a bookcase at the entrance to the master bedroom, replacing a set of French doors.

Below: Another pair of columns were added to showcase the view into the dining room.

Photos by: The Image Engineer

Built by: Classic Custom Builders

Kitchen

The catch-all for most anything, the kitchen was any man's territory. It's no wonder that assembling Hi-Fi kits, coloring Easter eggs and help-ing mom

bake, were right at home there. And because of its seemingly unassuming welcome to any and all, the kitchen holds an air of sacredness to us. The symbolic "center" of the home we grew up in, it drew us to the smell of

good food and an afternoon pot of coffee. It's a place that if we listen, we can still hear the echo of ourselves saying, "Hey Mom,

where should I put this?" And her uncalculated answer, "Just put it in the kitchen, for now."

Photos courtesy of: Lisa Olivo - Top & Bottom; Sheri Potter - Middle

THE MEDINAH MANOR

Built by: Carmichael & Dame Builders Inc.

Photo by: John Blackmer

9147-PC6

Dusky, dark dramatics.

An exterior crowned with quoins and stacked windows. The spirit of the kitchen dually meeting the breakfast area/family room and the butler area/dining room. The entry and living room visible from the balcony above. And a second-floor game room with walk-in closet and built-in desk.

Price Code: CD36   This home may have been altered from the plan's original design. For more information about the Medinah Manor refer to the index at the back of the book.

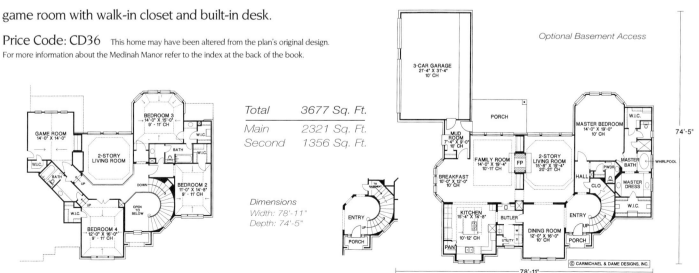

Total	3677 Sq. Ft.
Main	2321 Sq. Ft.
Second	1356 Sq. Ft.

Dimensions
Width: 78'-11"
Depth: 74'-5"

THE INGRAM

2281-PC6

Remnants of New England in a billowing flag.

When family drops by, a substantial great room and formal dining room. Both with shaped ceilings. Bayed breakfast area. And a master suite with amenities desired.

Price Code: 17   This home may have been altered from the plan's original design.
For more information about the Ingram refer to the index at the back of the book.

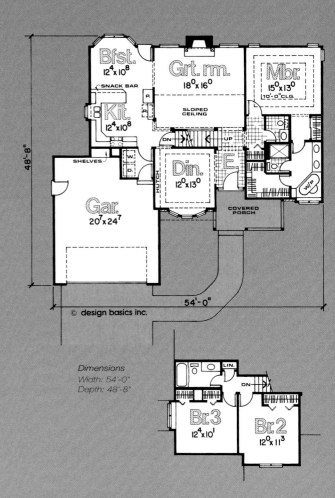

Total   1778 Sq. Ft.
Main   1348 Sq. Ft.
Second   430 Sq. Ft.

Dimensions
Width: 54'-0"
Depth: 48'-8"

THE ADAIR

2300-PC6

Built by: Tweedt Engineering and Construction

Attune to the sights of a warm dwelling.

Here, with a three-car garage. Dividing the dining room and breakfast area, a wet bar. With bedroom #3, the option of a den. A cathedral ceiling in the great room — lifting the spirit with its height.

Price Code: 14   This home may have been altered from the plan's original design. For more information about the Adair refer to the index at the back of the book.

Total Square Feet 1496

ALL PLANS *Customizable*

Dimensions
Width: 48'-0"
Depth: 52'-0"

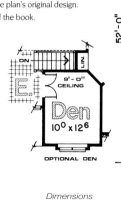

OPTIONAL DEN

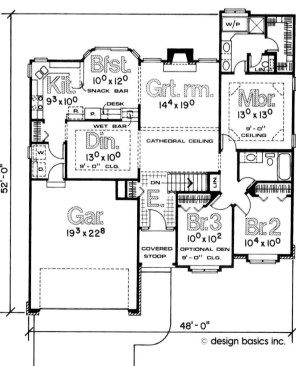

© design basics inc.

Built by: *Tweedt Engineering and Construction.*

THE CRAWFORD

2408-PC6

American blue and a wrap-around porch.

An integral part of our heritage, it seems. Bayed windows to the back and built-ins like an entertainment center and desk. A fundamental element to this home — the U-shaped stairway with a view of the entry and plant shelf. A vaulted ceiling, whirlpool tub and twin vanities, offerings in the master suite.

Price Code: 22   This home may have been altered from the plan's original design. For more information about the Crawford refer to the index at the back of the book.

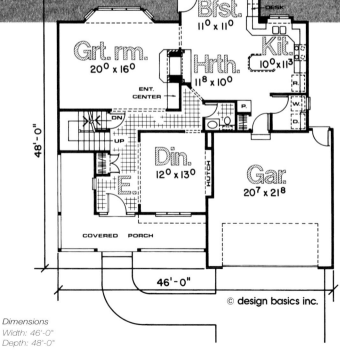

Bfst.
11⁰ x 11⁰

DESK

Grt. rm.
20⁰ x 16⁰

Kit
10⁰ x 11³

Hrth.
11⁸ x 10⁰

ENT. CENTER

48'-0"

Din.
12⁰ x 13⁰

Gar.
20⁷ x 21⁸

COVERED   PORCH

46'-0"

© design basics inc.

Dimensions
Width: 46'-0"
Depth: 48'-0"

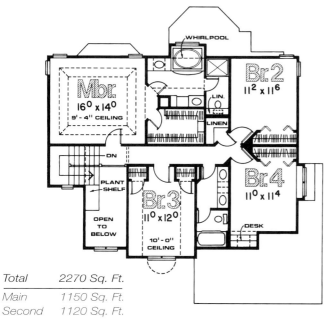

Total	2270 Sq. Ft.
Main	1150 Sq. Ft.
Second	1120 Sq. Ft.

Dining Room

It was, we assumed, the ritual of everything – the placement of the good china, silver and cloth napkins –

that exalted the dining room and made us all feel a bit more important, more sophisticated when present. For sure, there was nothing like eating holiday dinners there. Yet amidst the celebrated food and toasted wine, its significance was never completely made clear to us. We thought what made it special was the occasion, or the food and finery. What we never realized was that – with or without our Sunday's best – it was us.

Photos courtesy of: Carol Stratman - Top; Joni Vazzano - Bottom

Built by: Tweedt Engineering and Construction

THE ORCHARD

2818-PC6

A lazy summer day. A comfortable one-story to enjoy it.

Front and rear covered porches. Three-car garage.

Three bedrooms, or two with a den. A place to serve

meals to the dining room. And plain elegance in win-

dows draped about the great room and breakfast area.

Price Code: 16   This home may have been altered from the plan's original design.
For more information about the Orchard refer to the index at the back of the book.

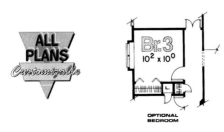

OPTIONAL
BEDROOM

Total Square Feet 1651

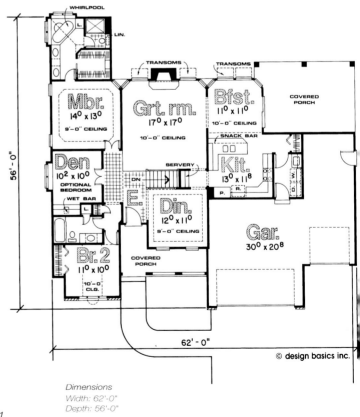

Dimensions
Width: 62'-0"
Depth: 56'-0"

© design basics inc.

THE DOVER

2376-PC6

A quiet demeanor.

Noticable nonetheless. A most-efficient design for the two of you. A second bedroom for such needs as a den. Shelves in the garage. Bookcase in the great room. Boxed windows in the breakfast area and master suite. All substantial benefits with strategic locations.

Price Code: 12   This home may have been altered from the plan's original design. For more information about the Dover refer to the index at the back of the book.

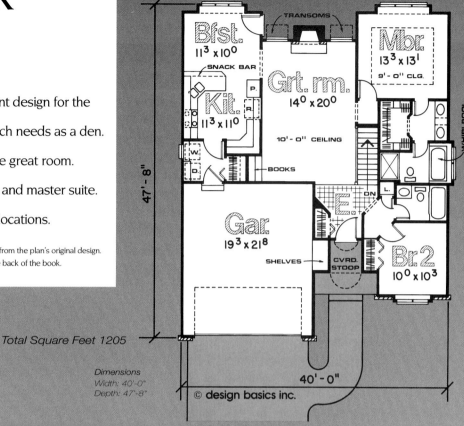

Total Square Feet 1205

Dimensions
Width: 40'-0"
Depth: 47'-8"

© design basics inc.

Built by: Landmark Homes

THE FAYETTE

2346-PC6

Perfectly executed proportion and balance.

Trimmed with subtlety. The stairway set on an angle to inspire one upon walking in. Living and dining rooms together — columns and tall windows poised for the formal occasion.

A fireplace and beamed ceiling making it hard to leave the comfort of the sunken family room.

Price Code: 24   This home may have been altered from the plan's original design. For more information about the Fayette refer to the index at the back of the book.

Total	2480 Sq. Ft.
Main	1369 Sq. Ft.
Second	1111 Sq. Ft.

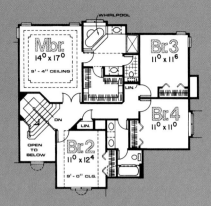

Dimensions
Width: 64'-0"
Depth: 46'-0"

© design basics inc.

Built by: Kendall Homes

THE TANNER

3249-PC6

Decisively traditional.

Three-car garage. See-through fireplace. Wide island kitchen setting off a bayed breakfast area. A window seat in the master bath. And a bonus room upstairs —to suit the individual desire.

Price Code: 22   This home may have been altered from the plan's original design. For more information about the Tanner refer to the index at the back of the book.

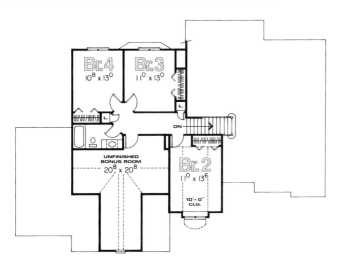

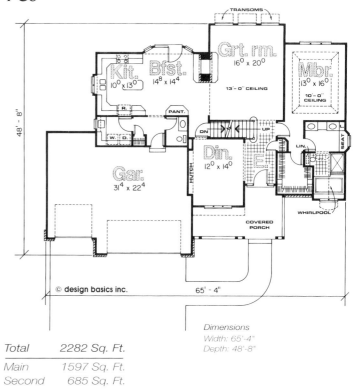

© design basics inc.

Total	2282 Sq. Ft.
Main	*1597 Sq. Ft.*
Second	*685 Sq. Ft.*

Dimensions
Width: 65'-4"
Depth: 48'-8"

THE CHURCHILL

2016-PC6

A dignified nuance of brick and siding.

An innate awareness of tradition, sophistication.

Walk-in butler's pantry near the dining room.

Luxuries in the master suite —a sitting room with

fireplace and a walk-in closet with two dressers,

skylight and iron-a-way. For the appreciative, a

second-floor display area.

Price Code: 39   This home may have been altered from the plan's original
design. For more information about the Churchill refer to the index at the back of
the book.

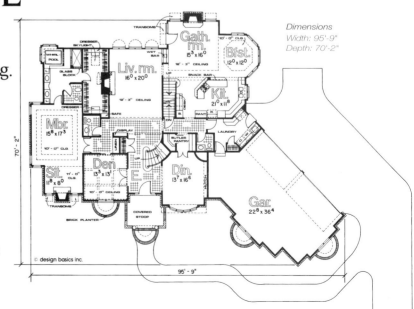

Dimensions
Width: 95'-9"
Depth: 70'-2"

© design basics inc.

Built by: Harold Taylor Homes

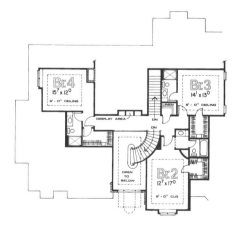

Total	3950 Sq. Ft.
Main	*2839 Sq. Ft.*
Second	*1111 Sq. Ft.*

Living Room

On the sofa we read our favorite magazines and made a rukus with our brothers. On the floor we played games at birthday parties and lay on our stomachs, chin in hands, watching "Leave It To Beaver."

True to its name, it was the place where we "lived."

Where we experienced lounging in a chair, munching popcorn. Where we posed for graduation and prom pictures, and unwrapped Christmas presents. A room that, day in and day out, brought us together as families.

Photos courtesy of: Priscilla Ivey - Top; Ann Leaders- Middle; Lisa Olivo- Bottom

THE ELDRIDGE

3064-PC6

Built by: Tweedt Engineering and Construction

A finished presence.

Born, perhaps, from identically gabled windows. Or its wide entry on the porch with thick, detailed pillars. An octagonal breakfast area specially placed to beckon from the great room and kitchen. The bayed dining room, just steps from the kitchen.

Price Code: 20   This home may have been altered from the plan's original design. For more information about the Eldridge refer to the index at the back of the book.

ALL PLANS *Customizable*

Total	2055 Sq. Ft.
Main	1414 Sq. Ft.
Second	641 Sq. Ft.

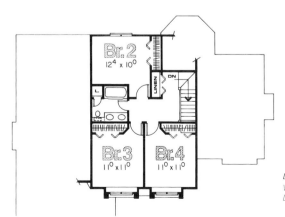

Dimensions
Width: 53'-4"
Depth: 50'-0"

© design basics inc.

THE HARRISBURG

2315-PC6

A stout Colonial with nice shape. Nice shade.

Living and dining rooms for tradition and familiarity. A generous bay in the family room and a pantry in

the kitchen. Noteworthy highlights upstairs — two bookcases and a nine-foot corridor ceiling.

Price Code: 19

This home may have been altered from the plan's original design. For more information about the Harrisburg refer to the index at the back of the book.

Total	1993 Sq. Ft.
Main	1000 Sq. Ft.
Second	993 Sq. Ft.

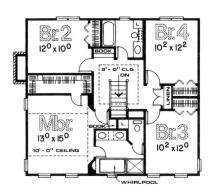

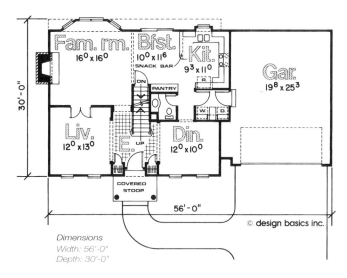

Dimensions
Width: 56'-0"
Depth: 30'-0"

© design basics inc.

Built by: Paradise Homes

THE EDGEWOOD

2839-PC6

A home of impressive accomplishments.

A sweeping stairway that creates a curved hallway between formal areas. Opportune for entertaining. French doors to a screened-in veranda, deep and unrestrained. An angling snack bar-meals in the breakfast area or snacks in the family room.

Price Code: 30 — This home may have been altered from the plan's original design. For more information about the Edgewood refer to the index at the back of the book.

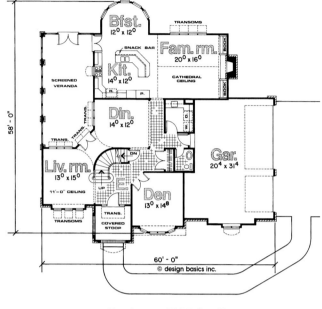

Dimensions
Width: 60'-0"
Depth: 58'-0"

Total	3057 Sq. Ft.
Main	1631 Sq. Ft.
Second	1426 Sq. Ft.

Built by: CPC Construction

THE PARNELL

3089-PC6

Scenery and silhouette speak of the South.

Georgia, perhaps. An interior side-load designed. But here, the garage adapted to the lot. A snack bar shared by the kitchen and breakfast area. Storage for whatever the need: in the garage and on the second floor.

Price Code: 17 This home was altered from the plan's original design. For more information about the Parnell refer to the index at the back of the book.

Total	1712 Sq. Ft.
Main	*1316 Sq. Ft.*
Second	*396 Sq. Ft.*

Dimensions
Width: 52'-0"
Depth: 59'-4"

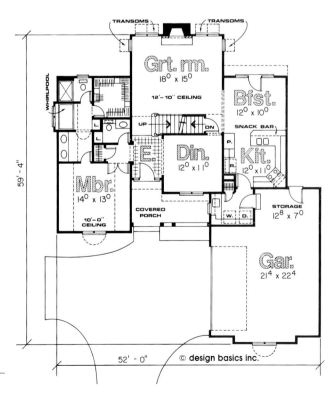

THE CANTERBURY
2411-PC6

Midnight influences. A magnified dance of purple, brilliance.

A private sitting room with bookshelves and fireplace, resting beyond columns in the master suite. Three upstairs suites, as well. Also on the second floor, an arched opening viewing magnificence in the great room almost 18 feet below.

Price Code: 36   This home may have been altered from the plan's original design. For more information about the Canterbury refer to the index at the back of the book.

Left: From the great room, a view of the second-floor catwalk and opened rear stairway.
Middle: The island kitchen has a view out a lovely bayed breakfast area.
Right: A fireplace flanked by windows in the hearth room.

Built by: M.D. Properties Inc.
Photos by: Dale Guldan

THE CANTERBURY 2411-PC6

Below: An elegant window adds character to bedroom #3.

Built by: M.D. Properties Inc.

Photo by: Dave Guldan

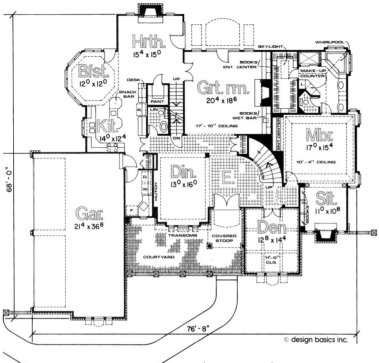

Total	3623 Sq. Ft.
Main	2603 Sq. Ft.
Second	1020 Sq. Ft.

Dimensions
Width: 76'-8"
Depth: 68'-0"

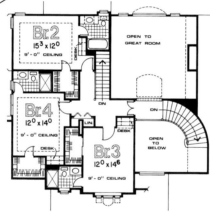

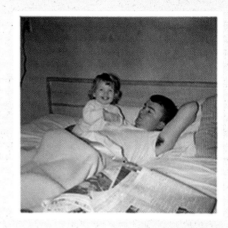

Bedroom

Unlike all the other rooms in your home, it was personal space. You went there to read, to crawl in with Dad or to finally have some privacy on the phone. It's where you played with your dolls as a child and isolated yourself as a teenager. The sacred place for your trophies, model cars and David Cassidy posters, nothing seemed quite as comfortable or as hard to leave in the morning. And even though you've long since moved away, it will forever remain - if only in spirit - strictly off limits.

Photos courtesy of: Carol Stratman - Bottom;
Cynthia Horan - Middle; Lisa Olivo - Top

Built by: Unique Homes
Photo by: Rob Lowe

THE LINDEN

2638-PC6

Proudly stacked windows and more above the front porch.

Lines and symmetry familiarly traditional. T-shaped stairway — just the thing when considering the second floor

from the kitchen or entry. From the upstairs landing, an aspiring view out the front or to the entry below.

Price Code: 21

This home may have been altered from the plan's original design. For more information about the Linden refer to the index at the back of the book.

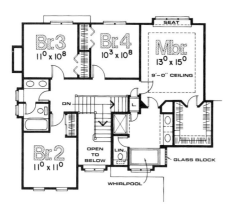

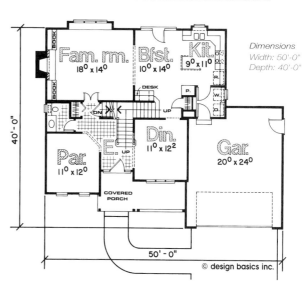

Dimensions
Width: 50'-0"
Depth: 40'-0"

© design basics inc.

Total	2103 Sq. Ft.
Main	1082 Sq. Ft.
Second	1021 Sq. Ft.

THE STRATMAN
3588-PC6

Simple styling reflected in clean, curved windows.

In storage above the garage. In the arched window and volume ceiling of the living room. Also, in a skylit master bath and wet bar for the family room.

Price Code: 21 This home may have been altered from the plan's original design. For more information about the Stratman refer to the index at the back of the book.

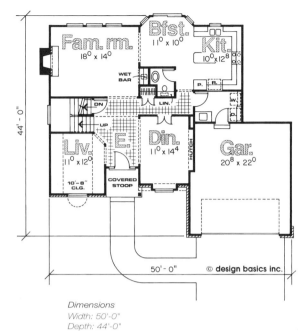

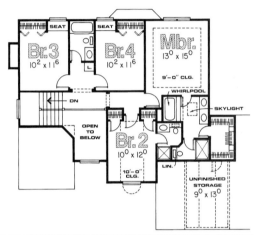

Dimensions
Width: 50'-0"
Depth: 44'-0"

Total	2198 Sq. Ft.
Main	1179 Sq. Ft.
Second	1019 Sq. Ft.

Built by: Ron Mahoney Builder

Built by: Southfork Homes

THE LOGAN
1551-PC6

An effortless one-story.

Sculptured boxed windows in front. Bright, informality in the dinette. A snack bar and desk there, also. Two secondary bedrooms inspired for those with hobbies. And in the master suite, the delight of a vaulted ceiling.

Price Code: 12   This home may have been altered from the plan's original design. For more information about the Logan refer to the index at the back of the book.

Total Square Feet 1271

Dimensions
Width: 50'-0"
Depth: 46'-0"

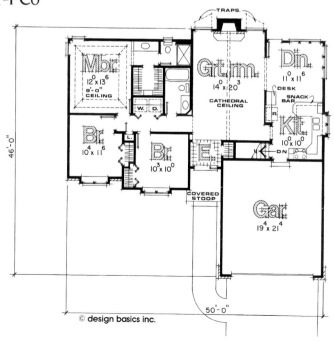

Built by: Southern States Construction

THE PINNACLE
3284-PC6

In the midst of dense greenery - grand stature.

Keystone accents on windows and entry. Lowered great room, set off by columns to the kitchen. A tall ceiling in the master bedroom, sloped on two sides. Behind double doors, a den. For private time away.

Price Code: 24 This home was altered from the plan's original design. For more information about the Pinnacle refer to the index at the back of the book..

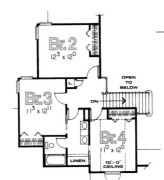

Total	2496 Sq. Ft.
Main	1777 Sq. Ft.
Second	719 Sq. Ft.

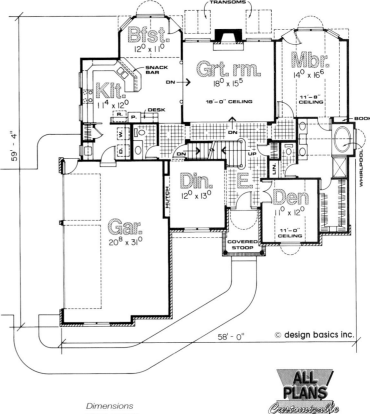

Dimensions
Width: 58'-0"
Depth: 59'-4"

ALL PLANS
Customizable

FAMILY LIFE ♫

A family is the beginning and the end of all things wonderful about home. It's most evident at times like this, where a picnic in the backyard becomes such a celebration, that it takes on the flavor of something much greater. Nobody won a soccer game or performed a perfect recital. It's not even anybody's birthday. It's just a family picnic, and afterwards, a game of tag and counting stars. You can see in their faces what they feel in their hearts — "We couldn't buy a greater time than kicking back with hot dogs and potato salad. We're a family."

SEP · 56

Built by: Southern States Construction

THE AMBROSE

2701-PC6

A warm, rusty brick.

Stucco naturally softened by greenery. Massive great room transoms trained on an exterior view. Built-in bookshelves and double doors to the den. A wet bar strategically placed between the great room and dining room. And space in the kitchen considerate for cooking.

Price Code: 23   This home may have been altered from the plan's original design. For more information about the Ambrose refer to the index at the back of the book.

Dimensions
Width: 56'-8"
Depth: 48'-0"

Total	2340 Sq. Ft.
Main	1701 Sq. Ft.
Second	639 Sq. Ft.

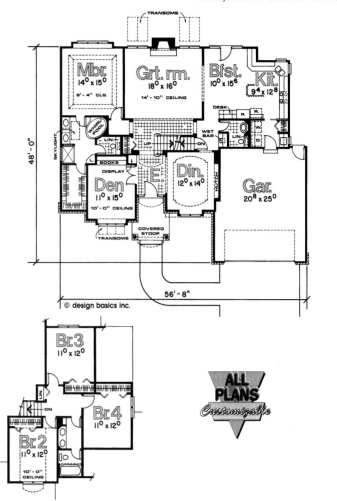

THE ASHVILLE
2811-PC6

The patriotic spirit of the farmhouse.

Perfected in white, with ruddy shutters. A comfortable dining room - less formal in its open appearance. Trapezoid windows and a cathedral ceiling clearly present in the great room. And an airy breakfast area. Made so by a 10-foot ceiling and bayed windows.

Price Code: 22   This home may have been altered from the plan's original design. For more information about the Ashville refer to the index at the back of the book.

Built by: Pacesetter Homes

Mbr. 16⁰ x 13⁰ 9'-0" CEILING

Kit. 10⁶ x 13⁰

Bfst. 11⁰ x 15⁰ 10'-0" CEILING

Grt. rm. 15⁰ x 20⁰ CATHEDRAL CEILING

TRANSOMS

Din. 12⁸ x 11⁴

WHIRL-POOL

Gar. 21⁴ x 22⁸

WRAP AROUND PORCH

54'-0"

52'-0"

© design basics inc.

Dimensions
Width: 54'-0"
Depth: 52'-0"

Total	2277 Sq. Ft.
Main	1570 Sq. Ft.
Second	707 Sq. Ft.

Br. 2 12⁰ x 12⁰

Br. 4 12⁰ x 11⁰

Br. 3 12⁰ x 11⁰

OPEN TO BELOW

8'-8" CEILING

PLANT SHELF

THE CYPRUS
2648-PC6

Clean. Crisp. Uniform lines sharing its subtle, polished effect.

The stairway, T-shaped for effortless traffic, open for a view to the entry. Twin bookcases, double doors and a boxed window in the family room. An elevated whirlpool. A shower under sloped ceiling. Magic touches in the master suite.

Price Code: 19   This home may have been altered from the plan's original design. For more information about the Cyprus refer to the index at the back of the book.

Built by: Tweedt Engineering & Construction

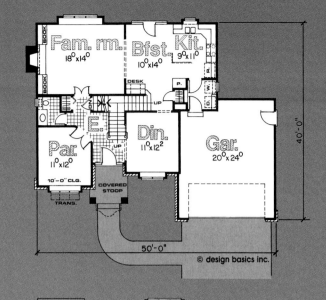

Dimensions
Width: 50'-0"
Depth: 40'-0"

Total	1951 Sq. Ft.
Main	1082 Sq. Ft.
Second	869 Sq. Ft.

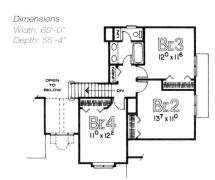

Built by: DCM Enterprises

Photo by: Kelly Mesenburg

THE ARANT

2261-PC6

A silhouette of form, finish.

Greetings from the dining room in the two-story entry. Within the living areas, a see-through fireplace and freedom to get around. A skylit vanity, sloped ceiling and significant whirlpool tub add luster to the master bath.

Price Code: 24   This home may have been altered from the plan's original design. For more information about the Arant refer to the index at the back of the book.

Dimensions
Width: 60'-0"
Depth: 55'-4"

Total	2405 Sq. Ft.
Main	1733 Sq. Ft.
Second	672 Sq. Ft.

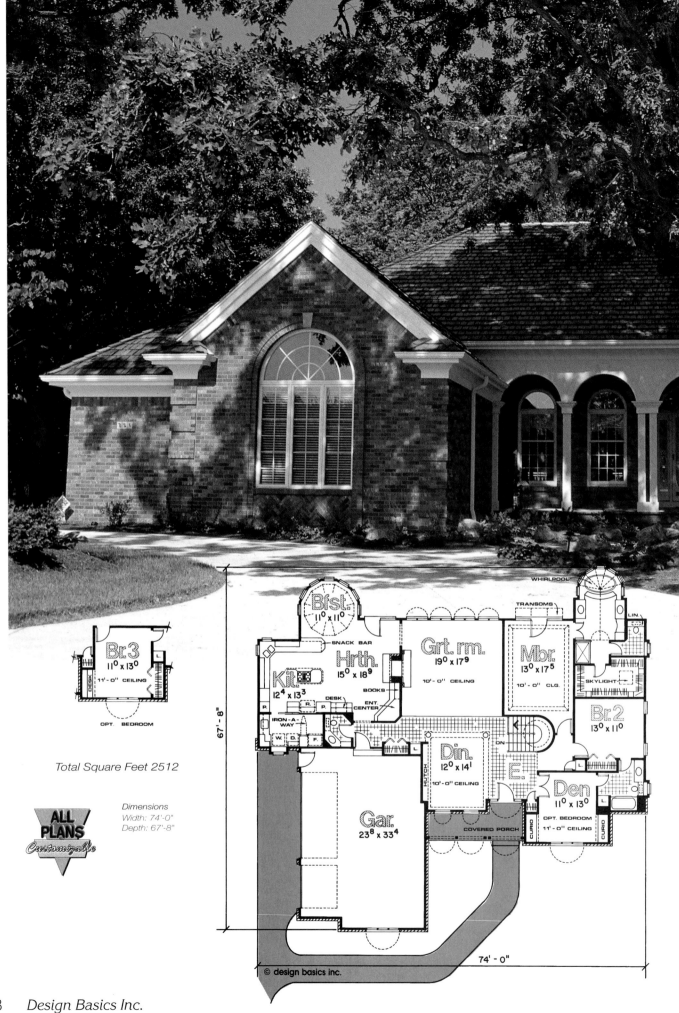

Bfst.
11⁰ x 11⁰

SNACK BAR

Grt. rm.
19⁰ x 17⁹

10'-0" CEILING

WHIRLPOOL

TRANSOMS

Mbr.
13⁰ x 17⁵

10'-0" CLG.

LIN.

SKYLIGHT

Br 3
11⁰ x 13⁰

11'-0" CEILING

OPT. BEDROOM

Kit.
12⁴ x 13³

Hrth.
15⁰ x 18⁹

BOOKS

ENT.
CENTER

DESK

P.

R.

P.

IRON-A-
WAY

W.

D.

F.

HUTCH

Din.
12⁰ x 14¹

10'-0" CEILING

DN

E

Br 2
13⁰ x 11⁰

Den
11⁰ x 13⁰

OPT. BEDROOM

11'-0" CEILING

CURIO

CURIO

Gar.
23⁸ x 33⁴

COVERED PORCH

67'-8"

74'-0"

© design basics inc.

Total Square Feet 2512

Dimensions
Width: 74'-0"
Depth: 67'-8"

ALL
PLANS
Customizable

Built by: Tweedt Engineering & Construction

THE LAWRENCE

2652-PC6

A perfect balance of shade and quiet.

A front porch, veranda-style with three airy arches. Two living areas - one, a hearth room with wrapping entertainment center and a place for books. Elegance inherent in the master suite: a whirlpool tub surrounded by windows under a dramatic ceiling. Also, his and her vanities and skylit walk-in closet.

Price Code: 25   This home may have been altered from the plan's original design. For more information about the Lawrence refer to the index at the back of the book.

Mom and Dad

Perhaps the best thing about them was the time they spent alone giving their complete attention to just you. Reading a book. Saying evening prayers. Goofing around in the living room. We relished these times because we knew that of all the other things they could or should be doing, they were, instead, with us - the only ones on earth they cared to be with at the time.

Photos courtesy of: Priscilla Ivey - Top & Middle; Lisa Olivo- Bottom

THE QUIMBY

3010-PC6

A pale sheen of refinement.

Hip roof, upon hip roof and a deep, arched stoop.

An arched opening again, to the bedroom wing

and two near the kitchen connecting the dining

room. Books for enjoyment by the dining room.

Gentle evenings on the rear covered porch.

Price Code: 14   This home may have been altered from the plan's original design. For more information about the Quimby refer to the index at the back of the book.

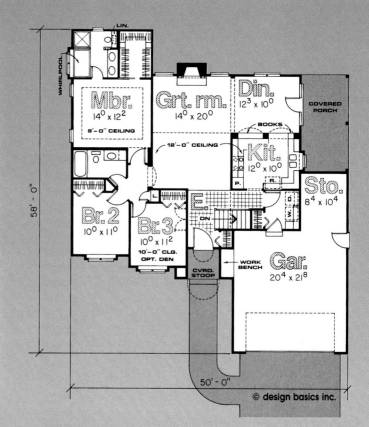

Total Square Feet 1422

Dimensions
Width: 50'-0"
Depth: 58'-0"

Built by: Southfork Homes

THE ASHWORTH

3103-PC6

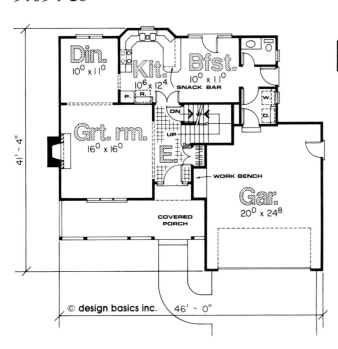

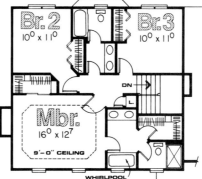

Total	1700 Sq. Ft.
Main	*904 Sq. Ft.*
Second	*796 Sq. Ft.*

Dimensions
Width: 46'-0"
Depth: 41'-4"

Simple emphasis. Charming effect.

Fluidity between the kitchen and dining room. The same when coupled with the great room and breakfast area. Three noteworthy others: A work bench in the garage. A wide dressing area in the master bath. And a front porch. For sipping, kicking back.

Price Code: 17   This home may have been altered from the plan's original design. For more information about the Ashworth refer to the index at the back of the book.

THE FRASER

2173-PC6

A quaint ensemble taking on a
sun-kissed luster.

Immediately upon walking in the door, a second

living space - suggesting a third bedroom, if needed.

Large kitchen pantry. Naturally brightened breakfast

area. A skylit master suite whirlpool. And a large

walk-in closet that's indented perfectly for a mirror.

Price Code: 14   This home may have been altered from the plan's original
design. For more information about the Fraser refer to the index at the back of
the book.

Total Square Feet 1451

Dimensions
Width: 50'-0"
Depth: 50'-0"

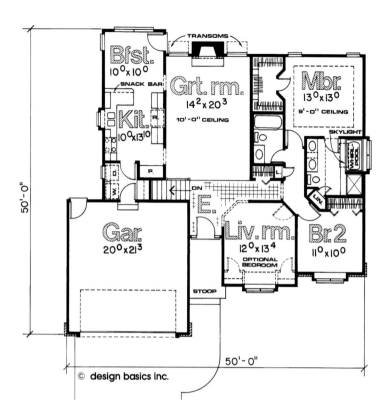

Built by: Maple Woods

Built by: *Muehling Homes*

THE PAIGE

3581-PC6

Personal expression.

Spider web detailing added for character. A place in the garage for bikes and the riding lawn mower. Between bedrooms #2 and #3, the option of a toy closet. Other indispensables: shelves in the laundry room. A coat closet in the entry. A central powder bath.

Price Code: 17   This home may have been altered from the plan's original design. For more information about the Paige refer to the index at the back of the book.

Total	1771 Sq. Ft.
Main	866 Sq. Ft.
Second	905 Sq. Ft.

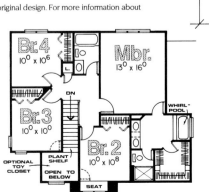

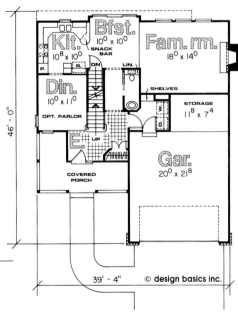

Dimensions
Width: 39'-4"
Depth: 46'-0"

Fam. rm.
16⁰ x 19⁴

Bfst.
12⁰ x 12⁰

Kit.
12⁰ x 17⁰

SNACK BAR

DESK

Liv. rm.
20⁰ x 17⁴

10'-0" CEILING

DRESSING

LIN.

DN
UP

Gar.
24⁰ x 21³

PANT.

BEVERY

WET BAR

DN

Dr. 2
13⁰ x 17⁴

10'-0" CLG.

BOOK'S

DN

LINEN

Br. 4
12⁰ x 15⁶

10'-0" CEILING

SEAT

DN

Br. 3
14⁰ x 15⁶

OPEN TO BELOW

Mbr.
19⁸ x 15⁰

10'-0" CEILING

Din.
14⁰ x 15⁶

HUTCH

E.

UP

BOOKS

Sit.
10⁴ x 13⁰

BOOKS

BOOKS

Gar.
24⁰ x 21⁰

STOOP

COVERED STOOP

Den
12⁰ x 13⁸

11'-0" CEILING

TRANS.

TRANS.

85'-5"

© design basics inc.

Total	3904 Sq. Ft.
Main	2813 Sq. Ft.
Second	1091 Sq. Ft.

Dimensions
Width: 85'-5"
Depth: 74'-8"

Top Right: Modification of the entry's design creates cased openings to the dining room and living room.

Middle: In the dining room, a detailed ceiling, space for a hutch and room for eight, if needed.

Bottom: A view of the Fairchild's rear courtyard.

Built by: Pridemark Design Inc.

Interior Photos by: Al Teufen

THE FAIRCHILD

2733-PC6

The dense, moody feel of a mansion in the English hills.

Quarried stone exterior. Comfortable and luxurious interior. Private sitting area just off the master bedroom.

Sunken living room showcased by elegant columns. The kitchen area - open to the casual atmosphere of a family.

Price Code: 39

This home may have been altered from the plan's original design.

For more information about the Fairchild refer to the index at the back of the book

THE FAIRCHILD 2733-PC6

Top:
His and her vanities were altered in the master bath to create one large, angled vanity.

Middle:
From the family room, a vista revealing the gourmet kitchen and bayed breakfast area.

Bottom:
The windows in the bayed breakfast area, altered to include arched transoms.

Built by:
Pridemark Design Inc.

Interior Photos by:
Al Teufen

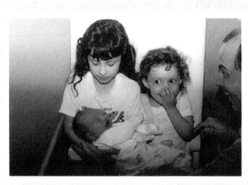

Baby

There has always been a special fascination in our hearts for the baby of the family. Our little brother. Our little sister. They came last, and more than likely, a few years later than the rest of us. In our minds they will always be little - "little Theresa" and "little Davy" - a stereotype they will carry with them forever. And though the years have now made them grown-ups like us, we still somehow find ourselves keeping an eye out for them, spoiling them rotten.

Photos courtesy of: Bruce Arant - Top;
Carol Stratman - Middle; Alva Louden - Bottom

Built by: Wayne Lesher Construction

Photo by: Wayne Lesher

THE HARTFORD

2458-PC6

Sleek stature. A wide, resting valley.

A rear covered veranda to take in the view. Three skylights and entertainment center in a vibrant hearth room. Three-car garage. And three second-floor bedrooms - with walk-in closets and nearby baths.

Price Code: 29   This home may have been altered from the plan's original design. For more information about the Hartford refer to the index at the back of the book.

Total	2932 Sq. Ft.
Main	2084 Sq. Ft.
Second	848 Sq. Ft.

Dimensions
Width: 68'-8"
Depth: 60'-0"

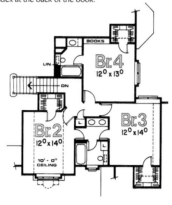

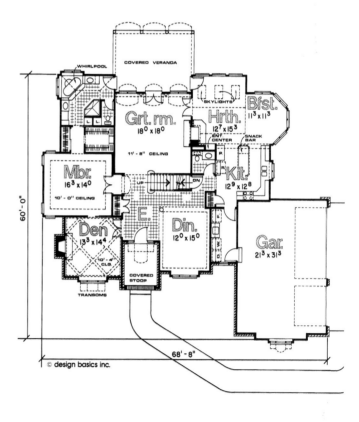

© design basics inc.

THE COMSTOCK

2778-PC6

Naturally integrated style.

A departure from the commonplace one-story. Transom windows illuminating the front and rear. Skylights on a covered porch. A sloped ceiling in the gathering room. A display niche in the entry. All adding a certain ease and beauty inside.

Price Code: 24   This home may have been altered from the plan's original design. For more information about the Comstock refer to the index at the back of the book.

Total Square Feet 2456

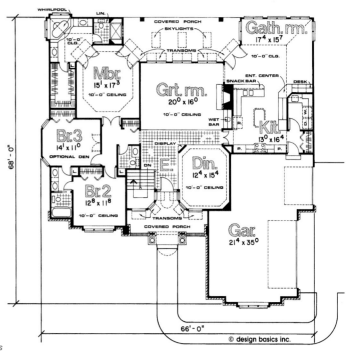

Dimensions
Width: 66'-0"
Depth: 68'-0"

Built by: Harold Taylor Homes

Built by: *Carmichael & Dame Builders Inc.*

Photo by: *Jeffery Hinds*

Total	4228 Sq. Ft.
Main	*2688 Sq. Ft.*
Second	*1540 Sq. Ft.*

THE SWEETWATER BEND

9119-PC6

A classic with an underscore of romantic freedom.

Space and light don the entry, gallery, dining room and two-story living room. Curved glass block in the master bath -

design inspired by the Japanese.

Price Code: CD42   This home may have been altered from the plan's original design.
For more information about the Sweetwater Bend refer to the index at the back of the book.

Built by: Dennis Smit Construction

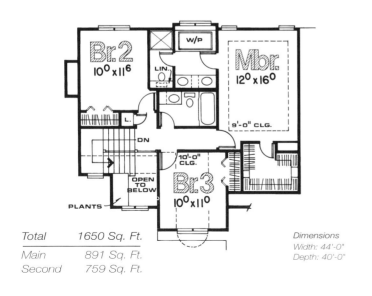

Br. 2
10⁰ x 11⁶

W/P

LIN.

Mbr.
12⁰ x 16⁰

9'-0" CLG.

L.

DN

10'-0"
CLG.

OPEN TO BELOW

Br. 3
10⁰ x 11⁰

PLANTS

Total	1650 Sq. Ft.
Main	891 Sq. Ft.
Second	759 Sq. Ft.

Dimensions
Width: 44'-0"
Depth: 40'-0"

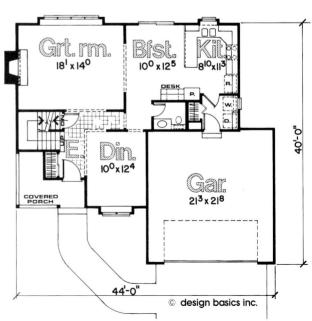

Grt. rm.
18¹ x 14⁰

Bfst.
10⁰ x 12⁵

Kit.
8¹⁰ x 11³

DESK

P.

R.

W.

D.

Din.
10⁰ x 12⁴

Gar.
21³ x 21⁸

COVERED PORCH

40'-0"

44'-0"

© design basics inc.

THE LAVERTON

2248-PC6

Shadows. Eminently soft and prone to make one wander out to the porch.

U-shaped stairway with a sloped ceiling and side window - for added effect when looking down at the entry. Boxed windows prominent in the great room. An arched window for effect in Bedroom #3. And the dining room - a Sunday dinner essential.

Price Code: 16   This home may have been altered from the plan's original design. For more information about the Laverton refer to the index at the back of the book.

Getting Together

If it was a meal, great.

If it was on the lawn, even better.

Both meant that you got to see Uncle

Ralph again and you got to tell the

joke you heard yesterday.

The whole group of you

meant something complete.

Most importantly,

it meant you were together.

Photos courtesy of: Cindy Steffensmeier-Top, Rita Hamele-Bottom

THE HAWTHORNE

2799-PC6

A timeless outward expression. A floor-plan with an equal profile.

The dining room window, truly inspirational. Warmth and ease in the kitchen, breakfast area and gathering room. And if desired - a finished basement with grand proportion.

Price Code: 18   This home may have been altered from the plan's original design. For more information about the Hawthorne refer to the index at the back of the book.

Total Square Feet 1887

Optional Finished Basement Adds 1338 Sq. Ft.

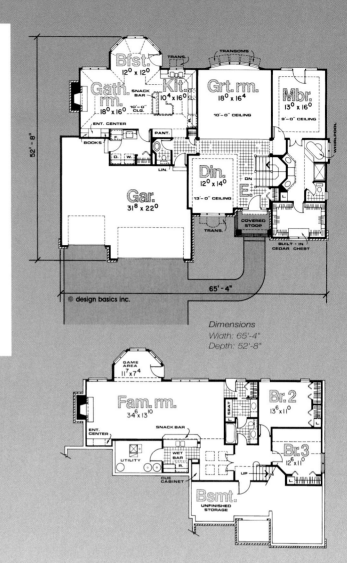

*Dimensions
Width: 65'-4"
Depth: 52'-8"*

Built by: *Unique Homes*

THE PAISLEY

2618-PC6

The addition of quaint details to harken the spirit back to the country.

Here and there, great things to help call it home: A covered porch. A bayed living room window. A detailed ceiling in the dining room. An island cooktop in the kitchen. And extra storage in the garage.

Price Code: 21   This home may have been altered from the plan's original design.
For more information about the Paisley refer to the index at the back of the book.

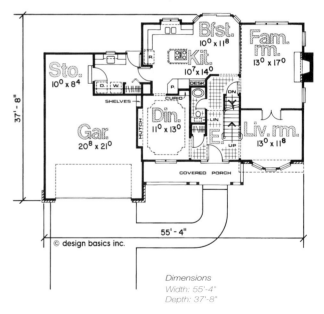

© design basics inc.

Dimensions
Width: 55'-4"
Depth: 37'-8"

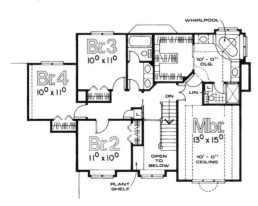

Total	2131 Sq. Ft.
Main	*1093 Sq. Ft.*
Second	*1038 Sq. Ft.*

THE MANSFIELD

1539-PC6

A definitive one-story home.

Designed with all brick originally, yet just as nice here, with only some. A choice of two spacious living areas or three bedrooms. And a tandem three-car garage for the boat, golf cart or '65 classic.

Note — two closets and skylight in the master suite.

Price Code: 19   This home may have been altered from the plan's original design. For more information about the Mansfield refer to the index at the back of the book.

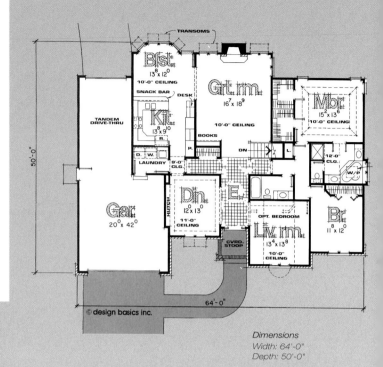

Dimensions
Width: 64'-0"
Depth: 50'-0"

Total Square Feet 1996

Built by: Demlang Builders

THE TYNDALE

2245-PC6

The green of summer on eclectic American architecture.

Two bedrooms upstairs. The master suite below - there, a skylit whirlpool tub and window seat to the front. Four long windows cornered in the great room.

Price Code: 16   This home may have been altered from the plan's original design. For more information about the Tyndale refer to the index at the back of the book.

Total	1685 Sq. Ft.
Main	1297 Sq. Ft.
Second	388 Sq. Ft.

ALL PLANS
Customizable

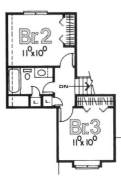

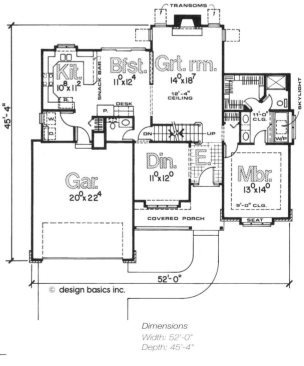

© design basics inc.

Dimensions
Width: 52'-0"
Depth: 45'-4"

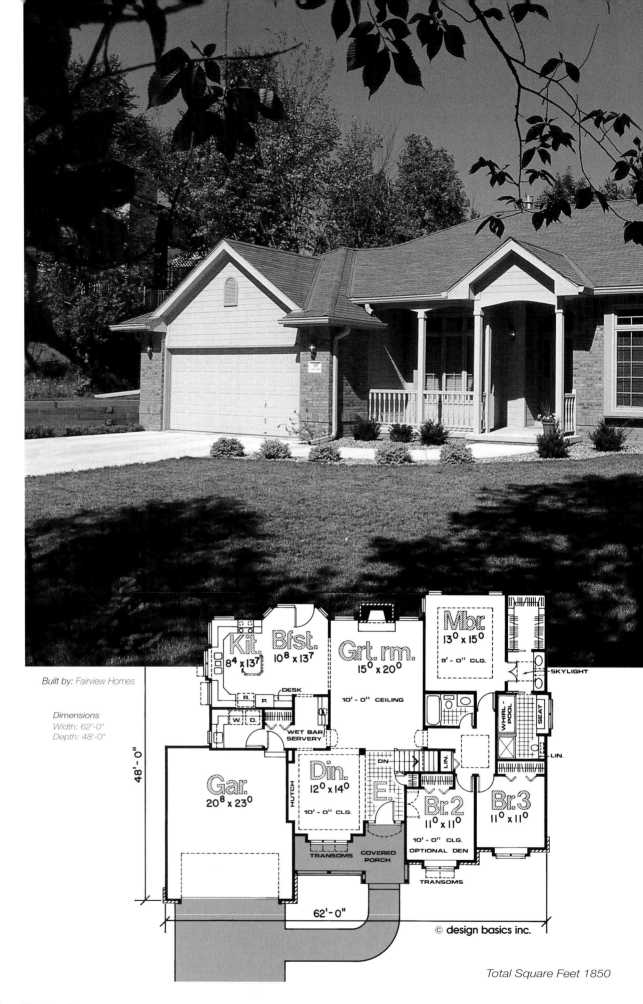

Built by: *Fairview Homes*

Dimensions
Width: 62'-0"
Depth: 48'-0"

Kit.
8⁴ x 13⁷

Bfst.
10⁸ x 13⁷

Grt. rm.
15⁰ x 20⁰

Mbr.
13⁰ x 15⁰
9'-0" CLG.

SKYLIGHT

DESK

10'-0" CEILING

WET BAR
SERVERY

WHIRL-
POOL

SEAT

LIN.

Gar.
20⁸ x 23⁰

Din.
12⁰ x 14⁰

10'-0" CLG.

HUTCH

DN

LIN.

Br.2
11⁰ x 11⁰
10'-0" CLG.
OPTIONAL DEN

Br.3
11⁰ x 11⁰

48'-0"

TRANSOMS

COVERED
PORCH

TRANSOMS

62'-0"

© design basics inc.

Total Square Feet 1850

THE SHAWNEE

2461-PC6

Sprawling. Sunny and laid-back.
Elements to retire to.

For the great room or dining room: a wet
bar/servery. Akin to spaciousness, volume ceilings
throughout the home. For some, comfort and
others, necessity - a skylit vanity and window seat
in the master bath.

Price Code: 18   This home may have been altered from the plan's
original design. For more information about the Shawnee refer to the index at the back
of the book.

Everyday Life

They are times that were never meant to
be seen. A Sunday in front of the tube.

Reba
and
Myrtle
dancing
in an
apron.

Soap suds
on a chin.
When
compared to
all other
moments
of family life,

most of these times are forgotten.
And yet, they are more
than worth remembering.

Photos courtesy of: Scott Silbernick - Top;
Rita Hamele - Middle; Sandi Webster - Bottom

THE PINEHURST

2311-PC6

Balmy brick and a cool Florida morning.

A view to nature through the entry, out the living room. An angled breakfast area transforming the gathering room. A master suite replete with built-in dresser, whirlpool and secluded access to the den.

Price Code: 24   This home may have been altered from the plan's original design. For more information about the Pinehurst refer to the index at the back of the book.

Built by: Shirah Builders

Photo by: Steve Shirah

Total	2486 Sq. Ft.
Main	*1829 Sq. Ft.*
Second	*657 Sq. Ft.*

Dimensions
Width: 68'-8"
Depth: 47'-8"

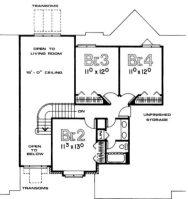

THE BRIARWOOD

2956-PC6

Hazy, moody and lush. Meticulous details with prominence.

Homework and paperwork in an office just off the kitchen. Columns and arches to the great room. Also, a sloped ceiling and more arched windows out the back. Such detailing viewed from the second-floor landing.

Price Code: 25 This home may have been altered from the plan's original design. For more information about the Briarwood refer to the index at the back of the book.

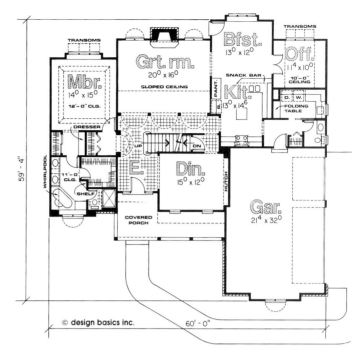

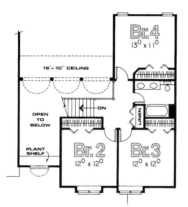

Dimensions
Width: 60'-0"
Depth: 59'-4"

Total	2562 Sq. Ft.
Main	*1875 Sq. Ft.*
Second	*687 Sq. Ft.*

Built by: Custer Homes

Photo by: Nicole Flemming

THE BARRINGTON WOOD
1035-PC6

The warm, rustic feel of wood.

A spider-beamed ceiling in the great room. The crackling appeal of the hearth room. The husky smell of a cedar closet on the second-floor. And a sense of quiet in the loft-like gallery.

Price Code: 29

This home may have been altered from the plan's original design. For more information about the Barrington Wood refer to the index at the back of the book.

Built by: Saddlebrook Designers-Builders

Photo by: Jeff Garland

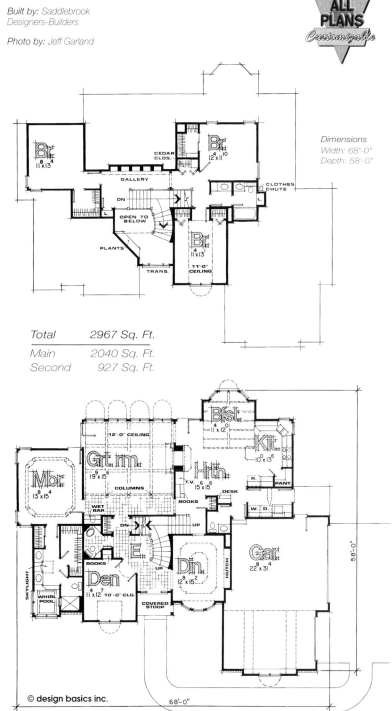

Dimensions
Width: 68'-0"
Depth: 58'-0"

Total	2967 Sq. Ft.
Main	2040 Sq. Ft.
Second	927 Sq. Ft.

© design basics inc.

THE AURORA
2836-PC6

Built by: Kahnk Homes

A perceptive elevation taking in the early morning.

Refinement in a wide, tiled entry spilling into the dining room and great room. An angled snack bar in a kitchen large enough for five. A small sunroom with French doors - perhaps a place to read or listen to the Eagles.

Price Code: 23   This home may have been altered from the plan's original design. For more information about the Aurora refer to the index at the back of the book.

Total	2308 Sq. Ft.
Main	*1654 Sq. Ft.*
Second	*654 Sq. Ft.*

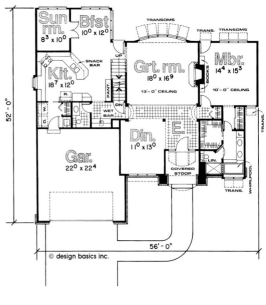

Dimensions
Width: 56'-0"
Depth: 52'-0"

SPECIAL OCCASIONS ᔕ

Within the vast archives of your memory stand out the very few days each year your family stopped to celebrate. Maybe you remember an especially wonderful Easter, New Year's Day or Fourth of July. All the same, every year you celebrated somewhere with people who were your neighbors, cousins and friends. You "aahh-ed" at the crimson explosion of the fireworks, toasted your kin at Christmas and sang "Auld Lange Syne" at midnight. These were meaningful times because whatever the day of the week, whatever the occasion, time was interrupted and placed on a shelf. A shelf that no one touched for the day, in order to honor the occasion. Like your eleventh birthday, when your Mom let you have a party and made your favorite cake with the special frosting. You and your friends drank soda pop and danced to your new '45 on the record player. And the home you remember, where all these things happened, celebrated the occasion right along with you. That's why whenever you think of this party, you will always think of home: the place of your best birthday ever.

Built by: *Semenza Homes*

Photos by: *John R. Dillon*

THE NEWBERRY

1455-PC6

Total	2594 Sq. Ft.
Main	*1322 Sq. Ft.*
Second	*1272 Sq. Ft.*

The blue of the sky. A wrapping porch.

The nostalgia of a simpler life. Formal and informal living areas. A sunroom

to fit your purpose. Four bedrooms paired with a laundry on the second

floor. And a play area for the children — or the child-at-heart.

Dimensions
Width: 56'-0"
Depth: 48'-0"

Price Code: 25   This home may have been altered from the plan's original design. For more information on the
Newberry refer to the index at the back of the book.

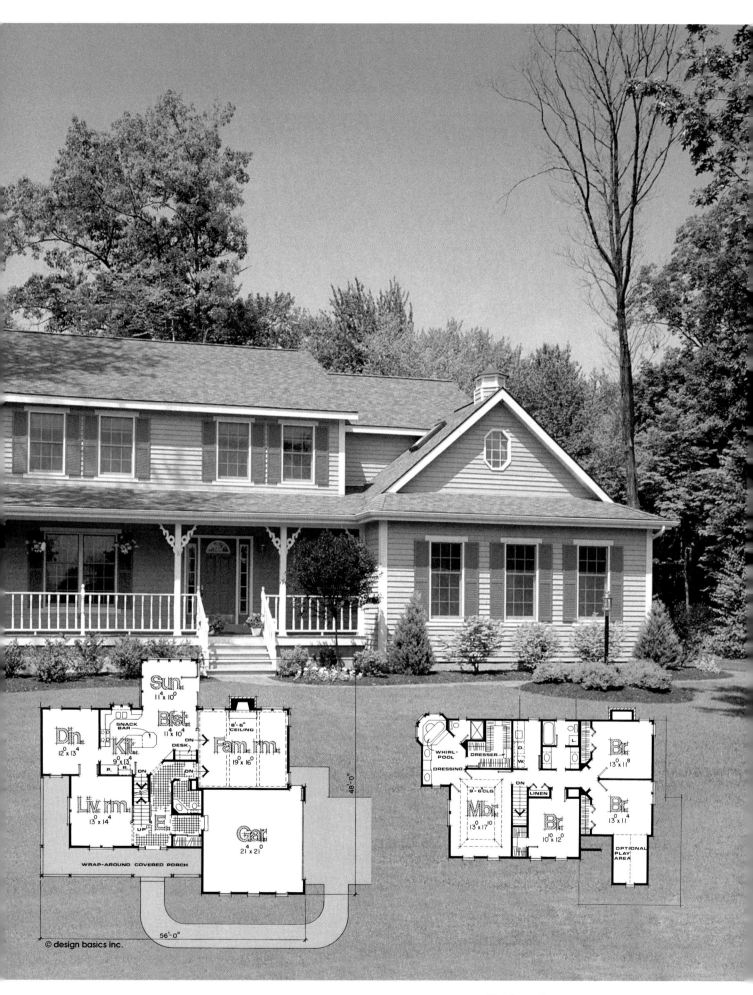

Sun rm.
11⁴ x 10⁰

Bfst.
11⁴ x 10⁴

SNACK BAR

Dn.
12⁰ x 13⁴

Kit.

9⁰ x 13⁴

DESK

8'-6"
CEILING

Fam. rm.
19⁰ x 16⁰

P.   R

DN

DN

Liv. rm.
13⁰ x 14⁰

UP

Gar.
21⁴ x 21⁰

WRAP-AROUND COVERED PORCH

48'-0"

56'-0"

© design basics inc.

WHIRL-
POOL

DRESSER

DRESSING

D. W.

Br.
13⁰ x 11⁸

9'-6 CLG.

LINEN

DN

Mbr.
13⁰ x 17⁰

Br.
10⁰ x 12⁰

Br.
13⁰ x 11⁰

OPTIONAL
PLAY
AREA

THE KAPLIN
1963-PC6

Enduring brick with urban appeal.

The master suite location, unnoticed. Included - a tiered ceiling, skylit vanity, whirlpool on an angle. And two other well-planned bedrooms to go with it. In the kitchen, more than adequate surroundings to store, cook and serve.

Price Code: 13   This home may have been altered from the plan's original design. For more information on the Kaplin refer to the index at the back of the book.

Dimensions
Width: 42'-0"
Depth: 54'-0"

Total Square Feet 1347

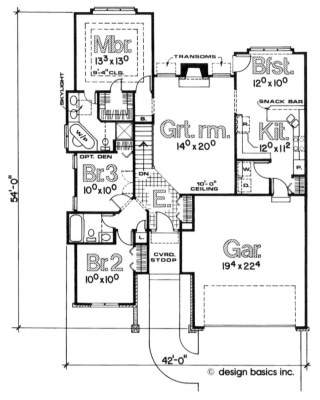

Built by: Landmark Homes

THE KINGSBURY

2445-PC6

A preferential home stated in mostly brick, with a copper-clad window and ornamental stoop.

For a formal audience, an elegant display of the dining and living rooms. Things that naturally go together in the great room and hearth room - bookshelves and a fireplace. On the second floor, over 200 square feet of storage.

Price Code: 28   This home may have been altered from the plan's original design. For more information on the Kingsbury refer to the index at the back of the book.

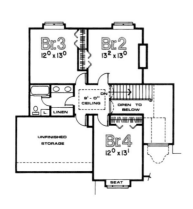

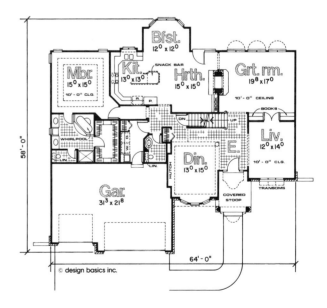

Total	2814 Sq. Ft.
Main	*2073 Sq. Ft.*
Second	*741 Sq. Ft.*

Dimensions
Width: 64'-0"
Depth: 58'-0"

Left: A view of the entry from the dining room.

Far Right: The lure of windows and a fireplace in the family room.

Right: A flood of natural light in the breakfast area and kitchen.

Built by: Homes Incorporated Builders and Developers

Photos by: George Gardner

THE MONTROSE

2127-PC6

A passion for pink. A passion for life in a notable home.

Living and family rooms expanded by French doors. Angled corridor secluding the master suite. Well-designed counter space, salad sink and snack bar — tailored to your needs in the kitchen.

Price Code: 22   This home may have been altered from the plan's original design. For more information on the Montrose refer to the index at the back of the book.

THE MONTROSE 2127-PC6

Above: The addition of a barrel vault ceiling in the master suite.

Photo by: George Gardner

Dimensions
Width: 54'-0"
Depth: 50'-0"

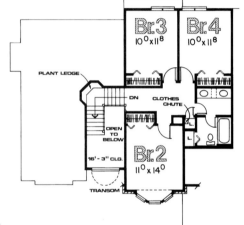

Total	2256 Sq. Ft.
Main	1602 Sq. Ft.
Second	654 Sq. Ft.

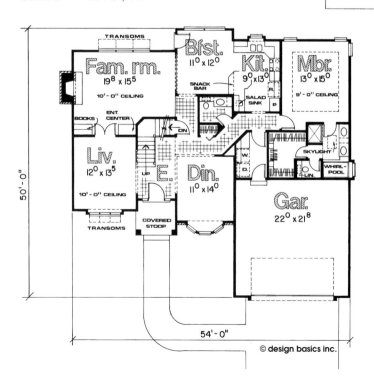

© design basics inc.

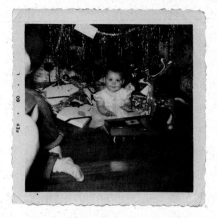

Christmas

The thought of barbie dolls

and paratroopers

turned your naughty into nice.

It was more than a day, it was a mood.

It meant carols and sugar cookies

and a whole season of anticipation.

You may have never roasted chestnuts,

but something about Christmas

has made you always want to.

Photos courtesy of: Heidi Pensyl - Top;
Sheri Potter - Middle; Leann Stungis - Bottom

THE CIMMERON
2215-PC6

An exquisite silhouette designed with brick and siding, but here built in stucco.

A pleasantly geometrical ceiling in the great room with built-in bookshelves. A sunroom with skylights and three sides of glass. Three arches draped about the entry of the living room - one for effect on the stairway.

Price Code: 28 This home may have been altered from the plan's original design. For more information on the Cimmeron refer to the index at the back of the book.

Built by: Michael Jacobson Real Estate and Construction

Photo by: Richard Pospisil, Jr.

Total	2854 Sq. Ft.
Main	1520 Sq. Ft.
Second	1334 Sq. Ft.

ALL PLANS *Customizable*

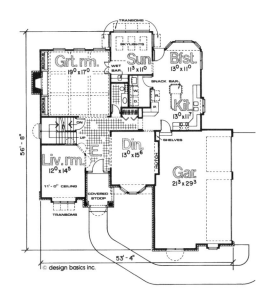

© design basics inc.

Dimensions
Width: 53'-4"
Depth: 56'-8"

THE BERMIER

2236-PC6

Graceful continuity.

Enchantment in a bright, arched window. A skylit whirlpool in the master suite. Optional storage on the second floor. And corner windows in the great room, tall and luminous around the fireplace.

Price Code: 18 This home may have been altered from the plan's original design. For more information on the Bermier refer to the index at the back of the book.

Total	1855 Sq. Ft.
Main	1297 Sq. Ft.
Second	558 Sq. Ft.

ALL PLANS *Customizable*

Dimensions
Width: 52'-0"
Depth: 45'-4"

Kit
$10^8 \times 11^2$

Bfst.
$11^0 \times 12^4$

Grt. rm.
$14^0 \times 18^7$
13'-8" CEILING

SNACK BAR

DESK

PANT

Gar.
$20^0 \times 22^4$

Din.
$11^0 \times 12^3$

Mbr.
$13^0 \times 14^0$
9'-0" CLG.

TRANSOMS

WHIRLPOOL SKYLIGHT

COVERED PORCH

45'-4"

52'-0"

© design basics inc.

Br. 2
$11^3 \times 10^3$

Br. 3
$10^0 \times 11^7$

LIN.

DN

OPTIONAL UNFINISHED STORAGE
$13^0 \times 13^4$

Br. 4
$11^0 \times 10^0$
10'-0" CEILING

Built by: Quality First Construction

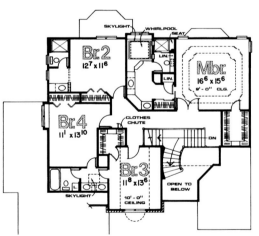

Dimensions
Width: 56'-0"
Depth: 52'-0"

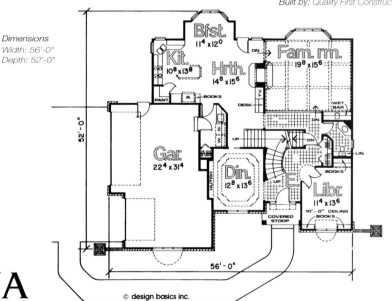

© design basics inc.

THE SANTA ANA

987-PC6

Total	3025 Sq. Ft.
Main	1583 Sq. Ft.
Second	1442 Sq. Ft.

A perfect day. A perfect two-story.

A sunken family room that shares atmosphere with the kitchen, hearth room and breakfast area.

Drama in the sweep of the staircase. Simply practical in its T shape. Airy in its open landing, overlooking the entry.

Price Code: 30   This home may have been altered from the plan's original design. For more information on the Santa Ana refer to the index at the back of the book.

THE LE GRAND

2218-PC6

Sultry on the outside with an inner, hidden agenda.

A sunken living room. Curved counter space in the kitchen. Convenient

servery near the dining room. A den so secluded you just might be able

to escape eternally.

Price Code: 36   This home may have been altered from the plan's original design. For more information
on the Le Grand refer to the index at the back of the book.

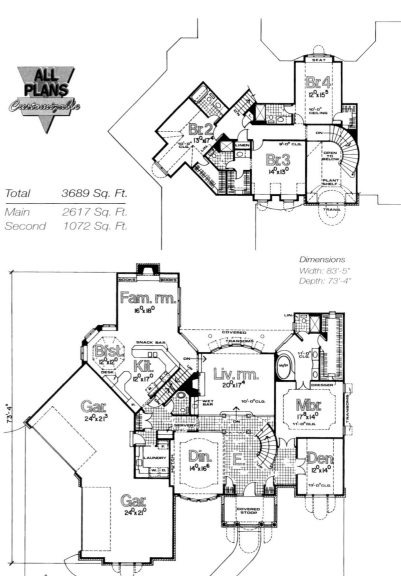

Br. 4
12⁰x15⁵

SEAT

10'-0" CEILING

Br. 2
13⁰x7⁴
10'-0" CLG.

LINEN

9'-0" CLG.

Br. 3
14⁰x13⁰

OPEN TO BELOW

DN.

PLANT SHELF

TRANS.

Total 3689 SQ. FT.

Main 2617 SQ. FT.
Second 1072 SQ. FT.

Dimensions
Width: 83'-5"
Depth: 73'-4"

Fam. rm.
16⁰x18⁰

BOOKS   BOOKS

Bfst.
12⁰x12⁰

DESK

SNACK BAR

Kit.
12⁰x17⁰

DN.

COVERED
TRANSOMS

Liv. rm.
20⁰x17⁴

11'-0" CLG.

W/P

DRESSER

Gar.
24⁰x21³

WET BAR

10'-0" CLG.

Mbr.
17⁸x14⁰
11'-0" CLG.

SERVERY

DN.

RANSOMS

LAUNDRY

W. D.

Din.
14⁰x16⁶

E.

Den
12⁰x14⁰
13'-0" CLG.

Gar.
24⁰x21⁰

COVERED STOOP

73'-4"

83'-5"

© design basics inc.

Left: The staircase in the entry – sweeping you to the second floor.

Built by: Decker Homes

Photos by: David L. Holman

Above: A detailed ceiling defines the dining room, with a half wall providing an open view to the living room.

Left: A kitchen's view to the breakfast area and beyond.

Below: The charm of the master bedroom.

Built by: Decker Homes

Photos by: David L. Holman

THE LE GRAND 2218-PC6

Easter

It was the Sunday that gave your
senses a sample of spring.
Ham dinners, sunrise services and
hollow, chocolate bunnies
were standard.
You were dressed in pastels.
You always matched.
And your Mom
brought out the camera
to capture it all.

Photos courtesy of: Scott Silbernick - Top;
Terri Vadovski - Middle; Dennis Brozak - Bottom

THE RENWICK

2230-PC6

Exquisitely finished details on a finely crafted, modern Colonial.

Note the exterior elements that make it so: crossheads, rowlocks, pediments and shutters. A spider-beamed ceiling and wet bar in the den entertain the great room. An oblique, octagonal breakfast area. Matching formal rooms. Three upstairs bedrooms - each with their own bath.

Price Code: 29   This home may have been altered from the plan's original design. For more information on the Renwick refer to the index at the back of the book.

© design basics inc.

Dimensions
Width: 72'-8"
Depth: 51'-4"

Total	2957 Sq. Ft.
Main	2063 Sq. Ft.
Second	894 Sq. Ft.

ALL PLANS Customizable

THE FRANKLIN

2316-PC6

Simple. Familiarly aesthetic.

Always nice to come home to. Continuity between the living and family rooms through French doors.

A master suite sitting room, whirlpool and entertainment center that advise nothing but escape.

Price Code: 23

This home may have been altered from the plan's original design. For more information on the Franklin refer to the index at the back of the book.

Built by: Paradise Homes, Inc.

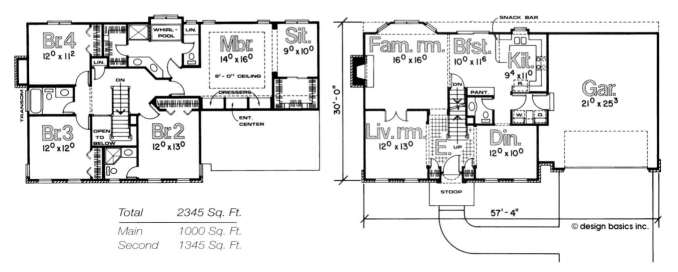

Total	2345 Sq. Ft.	
Main	1000 Sq. Ft.	
Second	1345 Sq. Ft.	

© design basics inc.

THE STANTON
2414-PC6

Built by: Tweedt Engineering and Construction

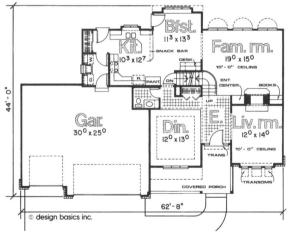

© design basics inc.

Dimensions
Width: 62'-8"
Depth: 44'-0"

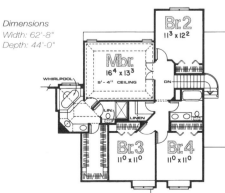

A designer's simplicity - clean and welcoming.

The living room, with space and light, an ideal partner for the dining room. Midway up the stairs, a view of three arches and a see-through fireplace in the family room. In the master suite, vaulted ceilings - an alternative to incite the imagination.

Price Code: 23   This home may have been altered from the plan's original design. For more information on the Stanton refer to the index at the back of the book.

Total	2343 Sq. Ft.
Main	1268 Sq. Ft.
Second	1075 Sq. Ft.

ALL PLANS *Customizable*

Built by: Miller Properties
Professional Builders

Photo by: Larry Umbras

THE HAZELTON

1019-PC6

Just the right shade of blue for an All-American home.

A tiered dining room ceiling. Storage in the garage. A great room with windows that naturally attract an outdoor view.

Price Code: 22   This home may have been altered from the plan's original design. For more information on the Hazelton refer to the index at the back of the book.

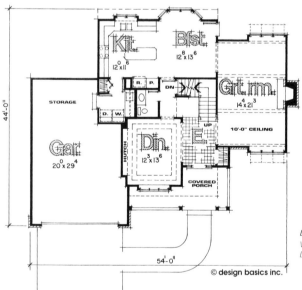

Above: Casual warmth in the kitchen and breakfast area.

Left: A splash of tradition in the great room, where windows flanking the fireplace were added to provide views to a near-by pond.

Built by: Miller Properties Professional Builders

Photos by: Larry Umbras

Note: The home shown was built in reverse of the original floor plan design.

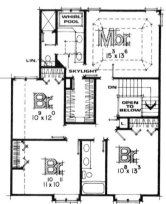

Dimensions
Width: 54'-0"
Depth: 44'-0"

© design basics inc.

THE HAZELTON
1019-PC6

Total	2219 Sq. Ft.
Main	1132 Sq. Ft.
Second	1087 Sq. Ft.

The Summer Holidays

Memorial day meant reunions.

The Fourth meant sparklers,

firecrackers and smoke bombs.

And Labor day meant just one more

ounce of fun before school started.

There was plenty of sunshine

and red-checkered table cloths,

along with the bonafide truth that

potato chips, fried chicken and cole slaw

just taste better outside.

You were guaranteed a mosquito bite

or two and for sure, a good time.

Photo courtesy of: Tammi Burbach

THE ELDORADO

2719-PC6

A handsome design, countrified, it seems, to compliment the sprawling prairie beyond.

A beautiful effect inside - angled windows in the 2-story entry matching the profile of the porch and shedding a notable amount of airiness. Kitchen, breakfast area and great room in agreeable combinations, each to enhance another.

Price Code: 19   This home may have been altered from the plan's original design. For more information on the Eldorado refer to the index at the back of the book.

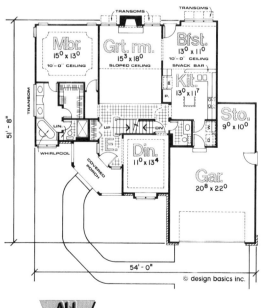

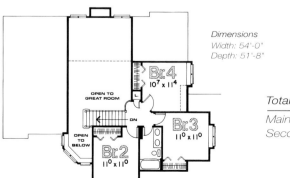

Dimensions
Width: 54'-0"
Depth: 51'-8"

Total	1976 Sq. Ft.
Main	1413 Sq. Ft.
Second	563 Sq. Ft.

ALL PLANS
Customizable

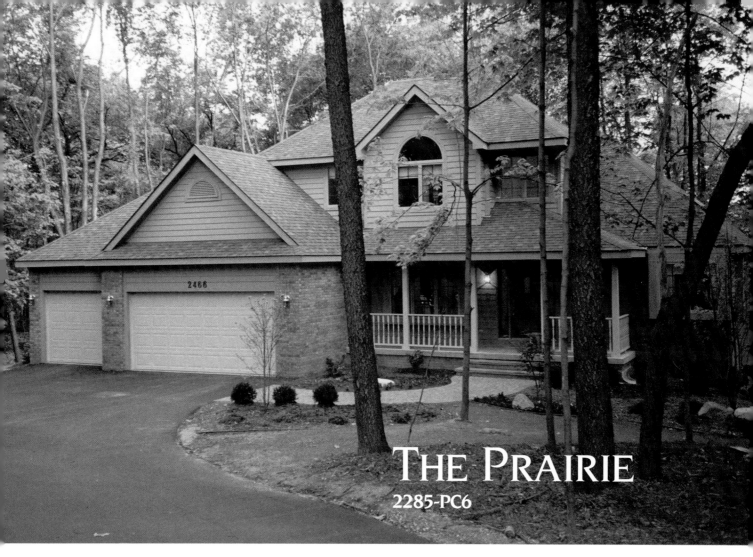

THE PRAIRIE
2285-PC6

Total	2115 Sq. Ft.
Main	1505 Sq. Ft.
Second	610 Sq. Ft.

Dimensions
Width: 64'-0"
Depth: 52'-0"

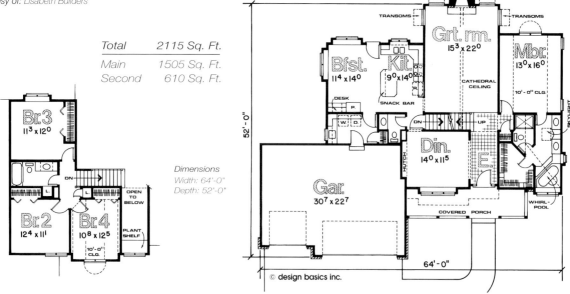

© design basics inc.

Just the right wooded setting for a home of this nature.

Cathedral ceiling in the great room. Sloped ceiling and skylight in the master bath. Snack bar island

in the kitchen. And things you should take for granted, like leisurely traffic from room to room.

Price Code: 21

This home may have been altered from the plan's original design. For more information on the Prairie refer to the index at the back of the book.

THE BALDWIN
2962-PC6

An array of graceful windows in late summer.

For today's family, a casual arrangement: an open T-shaped stairway and fireplace in the family room. Large entertainment center in the media room. Large corner pantry in the kitchen. Garage storage. And an elegant balcony - quite visible to the eye in the entry.

Price Code: 23 This home may have been altered from the plan's original design. For more information on the Baldwin refer to the index at the back of the book.

Total	2377 Sq. Ft.
Main	1206 Sq. Ft.
Second	1171 Sq. Ft.

Dimensions
Width: 52'-8"
Depth: 44'-0"

Built by: Falcone Enterprises

THE CORDEAUX
2174-PC6

Wearing the colors of Autumn with brilliance and charm.

A master suite off the beaten path. A living room that sees the family room
through its fireplace. Three large bedrooms that share two bathrooms on the
second floor. A staircase designed to be open and naturally light in its feel.

Price Code: 27

This home may have been altered from the plan's original design. For more information on the Cordeaux refer to the index at the back of the book.

Above: Two views of the master bath: twin vanities and the bayed whirlpool tub.

Photos by: Carl Saporiti

Dimensions
Width: 56'-0"
Depth: 59'-4"

Total	2708 Sq. Ft.
Main	1860 Sq. Ft.
Second	848 Sq. Ft.

THE CORDEAUX 2174-PC6

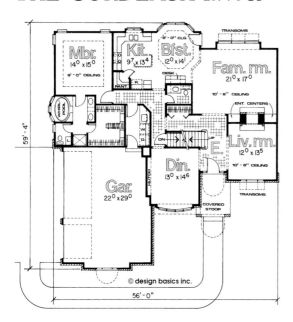

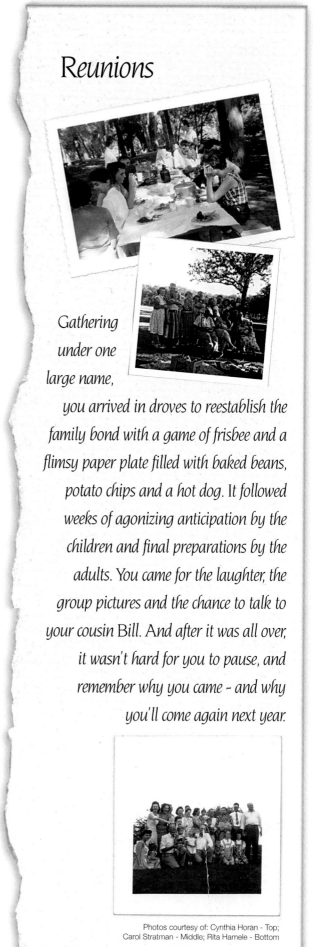

Reunions

Gathering under one large name,

you arrived in droves to reestablish the family bond with a game of frisbee and a flimsy paper plate filled with baked beans, potato chips and a hot dog. It followed weeks of agonizing anticipation by the children and final preparations by the adults. You came for the laughter, the group pictures and the chance to talk to your cousin Bill. And after it was all over, it wasn't hard for you to pause, and remember why you came - and why you'll come again next year.

Photos courtesy of: Cynthia Horan - Top; Carol Stratman - Middle; Rita Hamele - Bottom

Built by: *Mid American Building Corporation*

Photo by: *Mid American Building Corporation*

THE NEWMAN

1689-PC6

Indian summer light on contemporary angles.

Inside, a contemporary feeling too. An arched ceiling and columns in the entry. Diamond-cut dining room. The great room - opened with windows, the absence of walls and warmth from the fireplace. Also, a covered deck out back with louvered openings above.

Price Code: 21   This home may have been altered from the plan's original design.
For more information on the Newman refer to the index at the back of the book.

ALL PLANS *Customizable*

Dimensions
Width: 58'-0"
Depth: 74'-4"

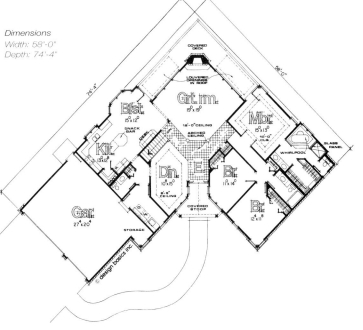

Total Square Feet 2133

Built by: J. F. Duggan Construction

THE BRISTOL

1870-PC6

Exquisitely executed in even tones, as it seems a Victorian should be.

Formal and informal living space with the freedom to move from living to dining as necessary.

Skylights and volume ceilings embellish the sleeping quarters upstairs, each with a strong

individual presence.

Price Code: 20   This home may have been altered from the plan's original design. For more information on the Bristol refer to the index at the back of the book.

WHIRLPOOL

SKYLIGHT   SKYLIGHT

Br. 3
11⁰ x 10⁰

Mbr.
12⁰ x 17⁰

DN

Br. 4
10⁰ x 11⁰

9'-0" CLG.

L.

Br. 2
11⁰ x 12⁸

11'-6"
CLG.

Kit.
10⁰ x 10⁰

Bfst.
9⁸ x 12⁰

Gath. rm.
17³ x 15⁰

DESK

R.

P.

DN

8'-8" CEILING

STORAGE

Din.
12⁰ x 12⁰

DN

Gar.
19⁴ x 22⁰

41'-5"

UP

Par.
12⁰ x 16⁴

12'-0"
CLG.

COVERED
PORCH

D.   W.

46'-0"

© design basics inc.

ALL
PLANS
Customizable

Total	2078 Sq. Ft.
Main	1113 Sq. Ft.
Second	965 Sq. Ft.

Dimensions
Width: 46'-0"
Depth: 41'-5"

Luminosity set off by the palest of early morning light.

In the family room: cathedral ceiling, twin entertainment centers and a snack bar that looks in the kitchen. A pair of windows in the master suite closet. An upstairs walk-in linen closet. A massive bonus room fortified with sloped ceilings and a triple-pane window.

Price Code: 27   This home may have been altered from the plan's original design. For more information on the Brennan refer to the index at the back of the book.

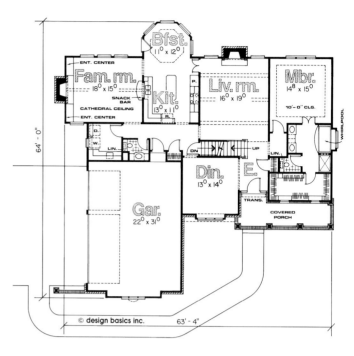

© design basics inc.   63'- 4"

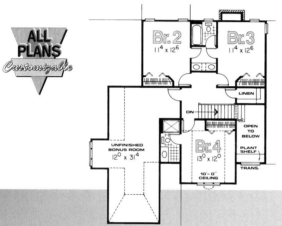

Total	2745 Sq. Ft.	Dimensions
Main	1921 Sq. Ft.	Width: 63'-4"
Second	824 Sq. Ft.	Depth: 64'-0"

THE BRENNAN
3493-PC6

Built by: Kahnk Homes
Photo by: Jeff Bebee

GROWING UP ∫∞

We were convinced of the usefulness of "things" – rubber bands, bottle caps and used tattoos from a Cracker Jack box. We traded comic books and baseball cards and spent most of our time in a world of make-believe. We were cops and robbers, cowboys and indians or the greatest superheros on earth. We were kids, wide-eyed, carefree and virtually animated with energy. We were so preciously young. It's yet to be determined exactly when it is, that time tells us to turn the page, past the days of kicking footballs and our first car. But, we have no choice and

somehow, we grow up. Today, we see our-selves in these, the universal faces of our youth. And when we look for that child again, we automatically think of home, the place where we never really lost our fascination for tree houses and dress up. We find truth in the memories of its kitchens, bedrooms and closets – the truth that says we will always be, if only a bit, what we were as children.

Photos courtesy of: Sheri Potter - Top Left; Cindy Steffensmeier - Top Right; Anne Bond - Bottom Left; Bruce Arant - Bottom Right

THE STERLING
1540-PC6

Calm colors that might go a bit understated if not for the generosity and depth of its windows.

Great bays in the dining and living rooms. Wet bar and see-through fireplace. In the master suite, a built-in dresser and skylit whirlpool — amenities that never seem to lose their appeal.

Price Code: 27   This home may have been altered from the plan's original design. For more information on the Sterling refer to the index at the back of the book.

Built by: Tweedt Engineering & Construction Inc.

Photo by: Rick Harrig

Dimensions
Width: 54'-8"
Depth: 52'-8"

Total	2727 Sq. Ft.
Main	1392 Sq. Ft.
Second	1335 Sq. Ft.

© design basics inc.

THE LEIGHTON

2377-PC6

Simple refinement in curves and choice of brick.

Stretched for a narrow lot. An expanse of entertaining space - the dining room joined unrestrictedly with the great room. In the master suite: access to a bookshelf. Tiered ceiling. Skylit vanity. Corner whirlpool tub. The solace of time alone.

Price Code: 16   This home may have been altered from the plan's original design. For more information on the Leighton refer to the index at the back of the book.

Total Square Feet 1636

Dimensions
Width: 42'-0"
Depth: 59'-8"

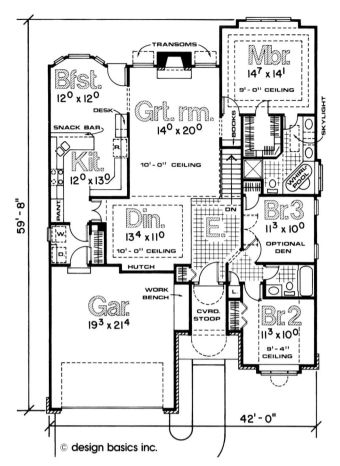

© design basics inc.

Built by: Landmark Homes

THE SIERRA
2745-PC6

Angles of interaction perfectly exposed from all sides.

Views start in the two-story entry, finish out the breakfast area and great room. Double doors to the master suite. There, volume ceilings. Transom windows. A built-in dresser or entertainment center. Bedrooms upstairs for three or more to sleep. One has the roominess of a 10-foot ceiling.

Price Code: 20   This home may have been altered from the plan's original design. For more information on the Sierra refer to the index at the back of the book.

Total	2089 Sq. Ft.
Main	1510 Sq. Ft.
Second	579 Sq. Ft.

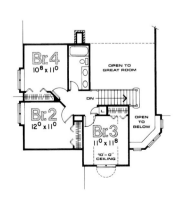

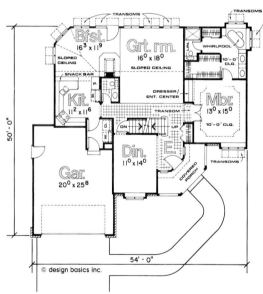

Dimensions
Width: 54'-0"
Depth: 50'-0"

THE MEADOWVIEW MANOR

9114-PC6

Bayed towers with a lofty ambition.

An amplified feeling of space in the dining room - its single wall a mirror. Other notable fundamentals:

game room, mid-level study, unfinished storage space and a blissful catwalk balcony.

Price Code: CD 41   This home may have been altered from the plan's original design. For more information about the Meadowview Manor refer to the index at the back of th

Above: The pure elegance of the living room.
Below: A long view of the gallery with striking display wall.

Built by: Carmichael & Dame Builders, Inc
Photos by: Richard Payne

KITCHEN
13'-0" X 18'-0"

UTILITY

F W D

10' CH

STOR.

PANTRY

DOWN TO BASEMENT

CAB.

4-CAR GARAGE
36'-6" X 21'-8"
10' CH

Optional Basement Access
(Makes overall depth 81'-0")

Total	4139 Sq. Ft.
Main	2489 Sq. Ft.
Second	1650 Sq. Ft.

Dimensions
Width: 72'-8"
Depth: 77' 0"

THE MEADOWVIEW MANOR
9114-PC6

Above: The beauty of arches defining the TV and curio cabinets in the family room.

Below: From the entry, a view of the two-story living room and catwalk.

Photos by: Richard Payne

Built by: Carmichael & Dame Builders, Inc.

Trikes, Bikes and Cars

You got the first for Christmas, the second for your birthday and the third for graduation. With each one, it seemed there could be nothing quite as grand.

They were shiny and they were your responsibility. They were your wheels, man. Each marked a stage in your life that meant something greater than getting around with a more advanced mode of transportation. You were growing up.

THE MANCHESTER

1862-PC6

Built by: Kendel Homes

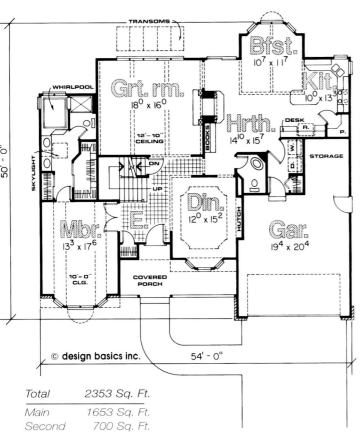

© design basics inc.

54' - 0"

50' - 0"

Total	2353 Sq. Ft.
Main	1653 Sq. Ft.
Second	700 Sq. Ft.

Rooms (Main): Grt. rm. 18⁰ x 16⁰ · 12'-10" CEILING · Bfst. 10⁷ x 11⁷ · Kit. 10⁰ x 13³ · Hrth. 14¹⁰ x 15⁷ · DESK · STORAGE · Din. 12⁰ x 15² · Gar. 19⁴ x 20⁴ · Mbr. 13³ x 17⁶ · 10'-0" CLG. · WHIRLPOOL · SKYLIGHT · TRANSOMS · COVERED PORCH · HUTCH · BOOKS

Dimensions
Width: 54'-0"
Depth: 50'-0"

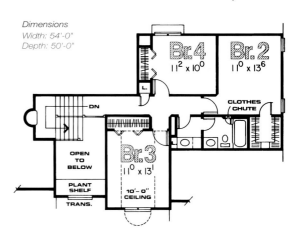

Rooms (Second): Br. 4 11² x 10⁰ · Br. 2 11⁰ x 13⁶ · Br. 3 11⁰ x 13¹ · 10'-0" CEILING · OPEN TO BELOW · PLANT SHELF · TRANS. · CLOTHES CHUTE · DN

Natural continuity in its line and detail.

Grace and ease in the entry that surveys the dining room and great room. See-through fireplace and bookshelf in the hearth room. The breakfast area, the place for a quiet meal and a piece of sunshine.

Price Code: 23 This home may have been altered from the plan's original design. For more information about the Manchester refer to the index at the back of the book.

THE WRENWOOD

3005-PC6

Bold colors entirely suitable to the setting.

The dining room, equally accessible to both the kitchen and great room. An optional den from bedroom #3. A computer den near the kitchen, but on second thought, perhaps a large walk-in pantry. Other elemental specifics: a wet bar; entertainment center; work bench; shower with two seats.

Price Code: 21   This home may have been altered from the plan's original design. For more information on the Wrenwood refer to the index at the back of the book.

Dimensions
Width: 64'-0"
Depth: 66'-0"

Total Square Feet 2186

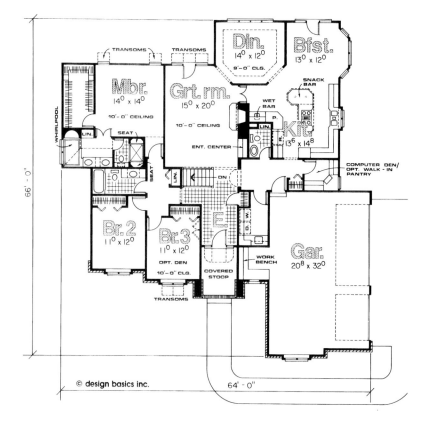

© design basics inc.

Built by: *Recic Homes*

THE MONTE VISTA

1032-PC6

Gracious curves and sweeps of brick.

The breakfast area made interesting by a valley cathedral ceiling and bayed glass. Separate bedroom wings for privacy. And brightness in the bath areas via skylights.

Price Code: 16   This home may have been altered from the plan's original design
For more information on the Monte Vista refer to the index at the back of the book

Built by: Tweedt Engineering and Construction

Photo by: Rick Harrig

Total Square Feet 1697

Dimensions
Width: 54'-0"
Depth: 54'-0"

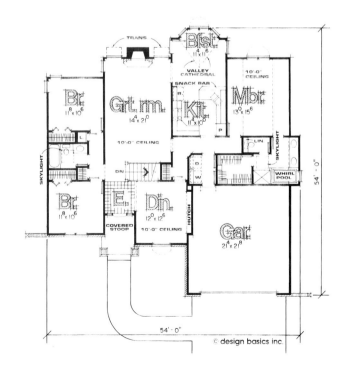

The rich texture of a southern Colonial and everything you'd expect inside.

An impressive great room, friendly to all areas of the home.

And a master suite beyond temptation.

Price Code: 34   This home may have been altered from the plan's original design.
For more information on the Carlton refer to the index at the back of the book.

THE CARLTON
1588-PC6

Built by: Saddlebrook Designers-Builders

Photo by: Jeff Garland

Dimensions
Width: 84'-0"
Depth: 52'-0"

ALL PLANS
Customizable

Total	3473 Sq. Ft.
Main	2500 Sq. Ft.
Second	973 Sq. Ft.

A Prized Possession

It was more than a cowboy hat, a scooter or a baseball bat.

It was your friend. It was security.

You took it to bed if you could. You barely let it out of

your sight while you ate. You remember the point in your life when you had to let

it go for bigger and better things. And now, you wonder what ever happened to it.

Photos courtesy of: Bruce Arant - Top;
Sheri Potter - Middle; Priscilla Ivey - Bottom

THE MEREDITH

2312-PC6

Built by: APCO Construction

Warm colors woven into a summer's day.

The living and dining rooms —formal profiles in the entry. In the master bath, extra room to move about.

On the second floor, a loft viewing the family room. And an option to expand over the garage.

Price Code: 21

This home may have been altered from the plan's original design. For more information on the Meredith refer to the index at the back of the book.

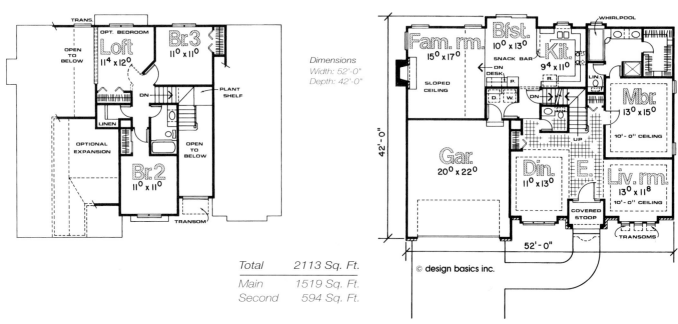

Dimensions
Width: 52'-0"
Depth: 42'-0"

Total	2113 Sq. Ft.
Main	1519 Sq. Ft.
Second	594 Sq. Ft.

THE LARAMY

3555-PC6

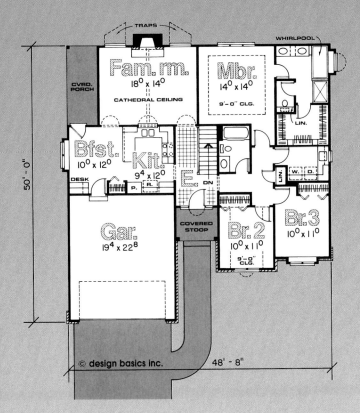

Something to revel in —
a palladian window set in brick.

Three arched openings in the family room. One viewing the

entry, another the breakfast area. The third over the kitchen

sink to see the fireplace ensconced between trapezoid

windows. To relax, a back porch.

Price Code: 15

This home may have been altered from the plan's original design.
For more information on the Laramy refer to the index at the back of the book.

Total Square Feet 1518

Dimensions
Width: 48'-8"
Depth: 50'-0"

ALL PLANS
Customizable

Built by: Cannon Construction

THE SAN BERNARD
940-PC6

A feeling of spring. A tree-filled lot. An affinity for brick.

Private access to the library from the master suite. Views from the second-floor catwalk. Two

skylights in the breakfast area and kitchen, supporting a natural attraction to the sun.

Price Code: 30 This home may have been altered from the plan's original design.
For more information on the San Bernard refer to the index at the back of the book.

Left: Changes in the great room opened up views to the rear - as seen from the second level.

Above: A glance into the library, here converted to a music room.

Built by: Crestline Homes

Exterior Photo by: Terri Richardson

Interior Photos by: Mark Rhodes

THE SAN BERNARD 940-PC6

Above: The skylit whirlpool and double vanity of a master bath designed to please.

Photo by: *Mark Rhodes*

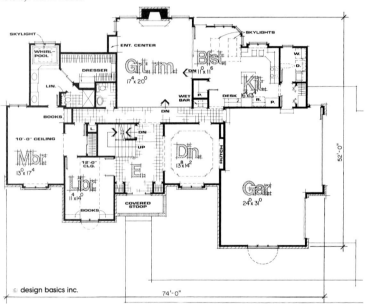

Dimensions
Width: 74'-0"
Depth: 52'-0"

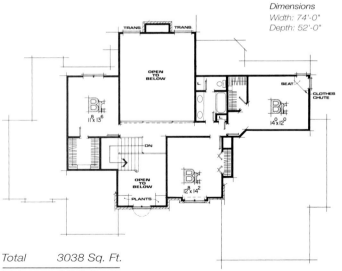

Total	3038 Sq. Ft.
Main	2078 Sq. Ft.
Second	960 Sq. Ft.

Brothers and Sisters

*They are those with whom
you are eternally linked
beyond time, reason or death.*

*It didn't matter if they were your age or
much older. Though you fought like cats
and dogs,
they were
still your
first, best
friends.*

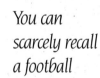

*You can
scarcely recall
a football
game in the front yard or a
sand castle at the beach without them.
Boy, what a time you used to have.*

Built by: Jerry Uhing Builders

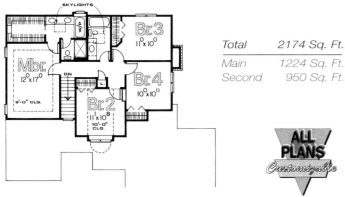

Total	2174 Sq. Ft.
Main	1224 Sq. Ft.
Second	950 Sq. Ft.

ALL PLANS *Customizable*

Dimensions
Width: 48'-0"
Depth: 48'-0"

© design basics inc.

THE COLLIER

2216-PC6

Rich brick and smooth curves suggest a perfect family home.

Two eating areas on either side of the kitchen, depending on the occasion. A sunken, unrestricted family room.

And a den to your suiting —an entrance from the front, or French doors to the family room.

Price Code: 21   This home may have been altered from the plan's original design. For more information on the Collier refer to the index at the back of the book.

THE CHANDLER
1554-PC6

Built by: Tweedt Engineering & Construction

Notably nostalgic from all angles:

Wrapping porch. Bayed dining room and breakfast area. Vaulted and skylit master suite. A staircase that bends at its mid-landing point — the perfect expression of an otherwise basic idea.

Price Code: 22   This home may have been altered from the plan's original design. For more information on the Chandler refer to the index at the back of the book.

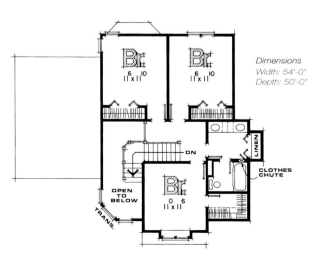

Dimensions
Width: 54'-0"
Depth: 50'-0"

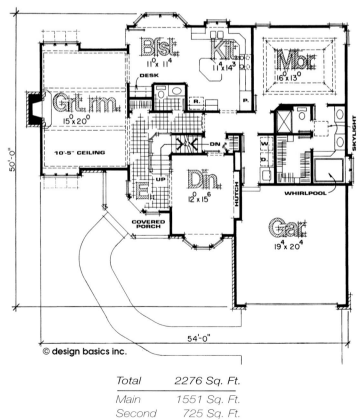

© design basics inc.

Total	2276 Sq. Ft.
Main	1551 Sq. Ft.
Second	725 Sq. Ft.

THE HANNIBAL
898-PC6

The gentle hand of yellow on a farmhouse.

A living room and dining room, fit for formal parties. Each also has access to complementing informal rooms to the back.

An iron-a-way and sink in the laundry room. Skylit master bath. And a two-story view in the entry

for the simple luxury of openness.

Price Code: 23

This home may have been altered from the plan's original design. For more information on the Hannibal refer to the index at the back of the book.

Built by: Dale Yost Construction

Dimensions
Width: 58'-0"
Depth: 40'-0"

Total	2360 Sq. Ft.
Main	1188 Sq. Ft.
Second	1172 Sq. Ft.

© design basics inc.

THE HAWKESBURY

2206-PC6

To see the three distinctive arches frame the front porch, is to feel something of this home's character.

Three bedrooms in a private wing — four if you convert the den. A family room for time together A living room that serves as the focal point of the entry — quite suitably.

Price Code: 24   This home may have been altered from the plan's original design. For more information on the Hawkesbury refer to the index at the back of the book.

Above: Green and luscious accents in the master bath.

Far Right: The open feel of the breakfast area and kitchen.

Right: A stunning view of the living room.

Built by: Grove Builders Inc.

Photos by: Brad Granzow

THE HAWKESBURY 2206-PC6

Above: The boxed ceiling and arched windows of the dining room.

Photo by: Brad Granzow

Total Square Feet 2498

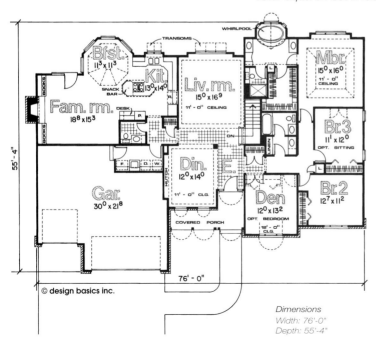

Dimensions
Width: 76'-0"
Depth: 55'-4"

© design basics inc.

Sports

Look ma you can see my spikes.

It was the roar of the crowd. The pungent smell of freshly cut grass. The shear physical determination of mind over body. You played for an opportunity to steal home and to hear the indisputable call of the umpire– "Safe!" You played in honor of

DiMaggio and Unitas and for your turn to humbly acknowledge your greatness to all. You played no matter the outcome and for the chance, to years later, safely boast to friends that "your" team was the greatest to ever have played at Washington High.

Photos courtesy of: Alva Louden

THE ASHTON
2203-PC6

Light tones and bright ideas.

Like a walk-in pantry in the kitchen. A living room

that opts as a den. And built-in desks in all three

second-floor bedrooms.

Price Code: 23

This home may have been altered from the plan's original design.
For more information on the Ashton refer to the index at the back of the book.

Total	2391 Sq. Ft.
Main	1697 Sq. Ft.
Second	694 Sq. Ft.

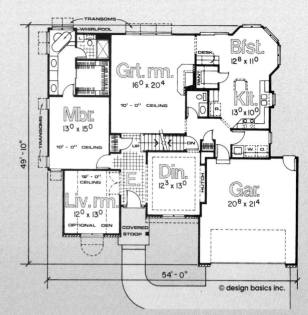

Dimensions
Width: 54'-0"
Depth: 49'-10"

THE KENDALL
1553-PC6

A simple two-story with crisp lines and an authoritative appearance.

Exuding this confidence —it's sleek arch-top and bayed window combination at the side. Two rooms to live in.

Two more to eat in. And a special preparation area near the kitchen —with a salad sink, no less.

Price Code: 23

This home may have been altered from the plan's original design. For more information on the Kendall refer to the index at the back of the book.

Built by: Tweedt Engineering and Construction
Photo By: Rick Harrig

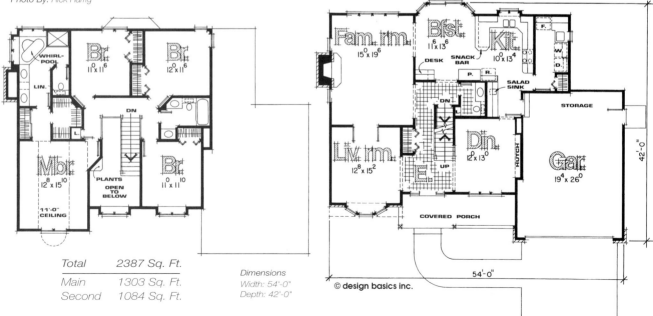

Total	2387 Sq. Ft.
Main	1303 Sq. Ft.
Second	1084 Sq. Ft.

Dimensions
Width: 54'-0"
Depth: 42'-0"

© design basics inc.

Built by: E & G Construction Unlimited

THE MONTEREY

2290-PC6

Casual in nature with an earthy blend of stucco and arches.

Volume ceiling in the great room.

Eating areas linked by the distance of a few steps.

A covered back porch to continue the tradition of a peaceful evening in the night air.

Price Code: 16   This home may have been altered from the plan's original design. For more information on the Monterey refer to the index at the back of the book.

Total Square Feet 1666

Dimensions
Width: 55'-4"
Depth: 48'-0"

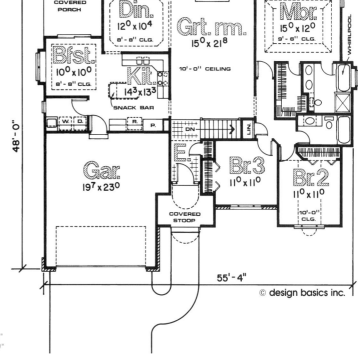

THE DUNDEE

2476-PC6

Filtering sunlight on a cheerful expression.

A columned, covered stoop meant to impress, but not to intimidate. The kitchen, breakfast area and gathering room — designated family space with built-in character.

Price Code: 28 This home may have been altered from the plan's original design. For more information on the Dundee refer to the index at the back of the book.

Built by: Saddlebrook Designers-Builders

Photo by: Jeff Garland

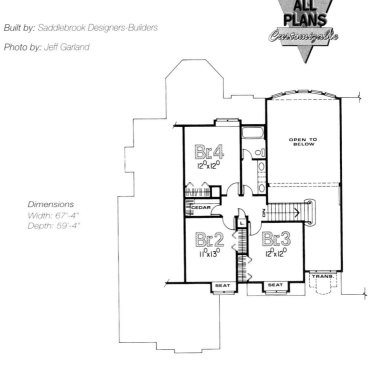

Dimensions
Width: 67'-4"
Depth: 59'-4"

Total	2884 Sq. Ft.
Main	2183 Sq. Ft.
Second	701 Sq. Ft.

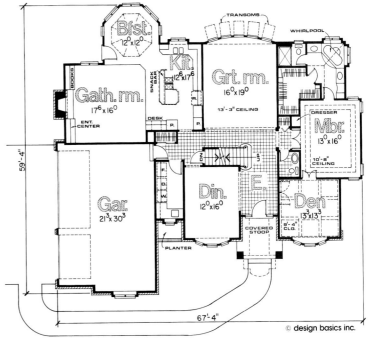

© design basics inc.

THE ROSEBURY

1767-PC6

A breezy, distinct design.

A see-through wet bar/servery shared by the dining room and breakfast area. Skylit master suite. Volume ceilings throughout for a feel that's notably open. And a look that's pleasantly different.

Price Code: 16 This home may have been altered from the plan's original design. For more information on the Rosebury refer to the index at the back of the book.

Dimensions
Width: 48'-8"
Depth: 48'-0"

Total Square Feet 1604

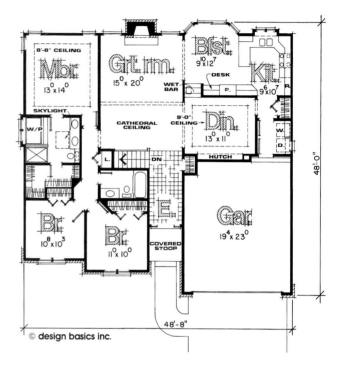

© design basics inc.

Built by: Tweedt Engineering and Construction
Photo By: Rick Harrig

SPECIAL PEOPLE ⌐

They were witty and elegant, enduring and wise, and not entirely predictable. Your thoughts of home reflect a bit of their personality. They were the people you admired for their spirit which in many ways has taken over yours. You've adopted their charm, their fire for life or their kind, compassionate ways. You've elevated them to heroes that saved the day. And even if they didn't have the answers, they always somehow made you feel better. People like your high school English teacher. Your best friend. Or your grandfather who smelled of gingersnaps and tobacco, tickled your toes when he put on your socks and made a point to take you up on his lap at each visit. Such people touched your life when you least expected it and left your life too soon. Or perhaps they're still here, in which case there's yet time to thank them for taking a hold of your heart and never really giving it back.

THE PATERSON

1380-PC6

Built by: Overholser Builders

Total	1999 Sq. Ft.
Main	1421 Sq. Ft.
Second	578 Sq. Ft.

Dimensions
Width: 52'-0"
Depth: 47'-4"

Always a great combination: pretty and popular.

Unforgettable windows in all major rooms. See-through fireplace. Easy traffic

from garage to kitchen. All of these, adaptations for a modern lifestyle.

Price Code: 19   This home may have been altered from the plan's original design.

For more information on the Paterson refer to the index at the back of the book.

THE EASTGATE

2406-PC6

Mbr.
18⁸ x 17⁴
11' - 0" CEILING

Liv. rm.
16⁰ x 20⁰
11' - 0" CEILING
WET BAR

Bfst
12⁰ x 12⁰
SNACK BAR

Kit.
16⁰ x 16⁰
PANTRY
PANTRY
DESK

Fam. rm.
18⁰ x 19³
11' - 0" CEILING

Br. 2
12⁰ x 15²

DRESSER
SEAT
DRESSING
BOOKS
GALLERY
LIN.
LAUNDRY

Din.
13⁰ x 16⁰
SHELVES
HUTCH

COVERED VERANDA

Den.
12⁷ x 17⁸
12' - 0" CEILING

COVERED STOOP

Gar.
21³ x 38⁰

UNFINISHED STORAGE

OPEN TO BELOW

Br 3
12⁰ x 15⁰
10' - 0" CEILING

BOOKS
LINEN

Br 4
14⁰ x 12⁰
SHELVES

72' - 0"

© design basics inc.

Total	3827 Sq. Ft.
Main	*2789 Sq. Ft.*
Second	*1038 Sq. Ft.*

Top: The fluidity of the curved staircase in the entry.

Middle: His and her vanities and a corner whirlpool tub to define the master bath.

Bottom: A view of the comfortable den, here as a sitting room.

Built by: Oak Tree Homes

Photos by: Tom Weigand

Dimensions
Width: 72'-0"
Depth: 73'-4"

Sun-washed richness.

A handsome definition of color, detail. Two staircases — one sweeping the entry and the other neatly tucked in the kitchen. A snack bar large enough to seat everyone from the family room. And a covered veranda — private to an inviting master suite.

Price Code: 38   This home may have been altered from the plan's original design.
For more information on the Eastgate refer to the index at the back of the book.

Built by: Bilstad Building Inc.

THE ABBEY

1510-PC6

Tradition borrowed from the English manor.

A large, airy kitchen. Combined formal rooms.

A private library with built-in bookshelves. On the

second floor, a clothes chute. Volume ceilings. A

private sitting room. Everyday, unbridled luxuries.

Price Code: 33   This home may have been altered from the plan's
original design. For more information on the Abbey refer to the index at the back
of the book.

© design basics inc.

Pals

Together as dragon-slayers, secret spies

and the most feared pirates of the sea,

you conquered every inch of each others' houses.

As princesses and mommies

you had the best tea parties in town.

It never crossed your minds that

you might someday live a thousand miles apart

because at the time,

you thought you couldn't do anything

without each other.

Photos courtesy of: Bruce Arant - Top; Alva Louden - Bottom

Dimensions
Width: 62'-0"
Depth: 55'-4"

Total	*3306 Sq. Ft.*
Main	*1709 Sq. Ft.*
Second	*1597 Sq. Ft.*

THE BARTELS

2579-PC6

A snug, bungalow-inspired two-story.

An intricate living room with angled entrance, cathedral ceiling, fireplace and tall corner windows. An island kitchen. Neat breakfast area. And an enclosed den that's composed, enlightened with windows. In two second - floor bedrooms — double doors for one and a window seat for another.

Price Code: 15

This home may have been altered from the plan's original design. For more information on the Bartels refer to the index at the back of the book.

Total	1594 Sq. Ft.
Main	869 Sq. Ft.
Second	725 Sq. Ft.

Dimensions
Width: 38'-0"
Depth: 44'-4"

THE NEWPORT

2293-PC6

Built by: Kahnk Homes

Early Autumn light on a Design Basics classic.

Central staircase with dual-access. Volume ceiling and bayed sitting area in the master suite.

Two large living areas where the comforts of home are the preference.

Price Code: 28

This home may have been altered from the plan's original design. For more information on the Newport refer to the index at the back of the book.

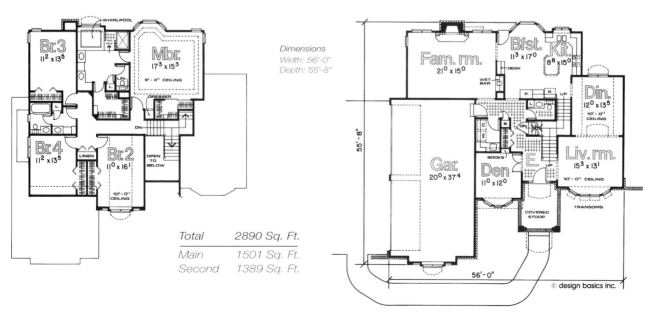

Dimensions
Width: 56'-0"
Depth: 55'-8"

Total	2890 Sq. Ft.
Main	1501 Sq. Ft.
Second	1389 Sq. Ft.

© design basics inc.

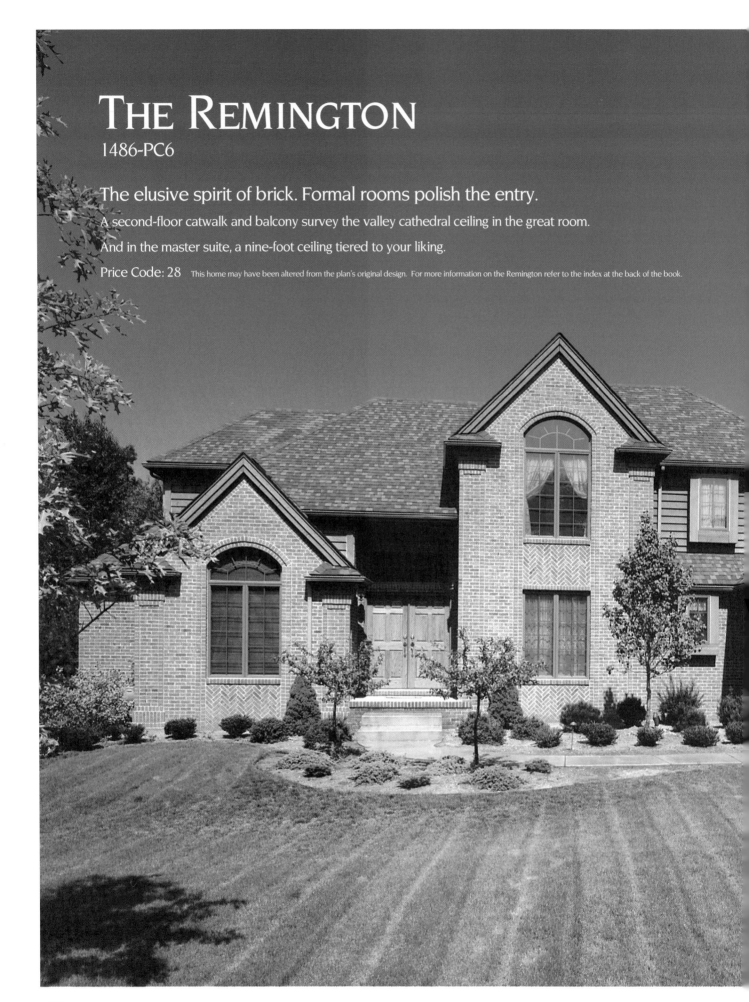

THE REMINGTON

1486-PC6

The elusive spirit of brick. Formal rooms polish the entry.

A second-floor catwalk and balcony survey the valley cathedral ceiling in the great room.

And in the master suite, a nine-foot ceiling tiered to your liking.

Price Code: 28   This home may have been altered from the plan's original design. For more information on the Remington refer to the index at the back of the book.

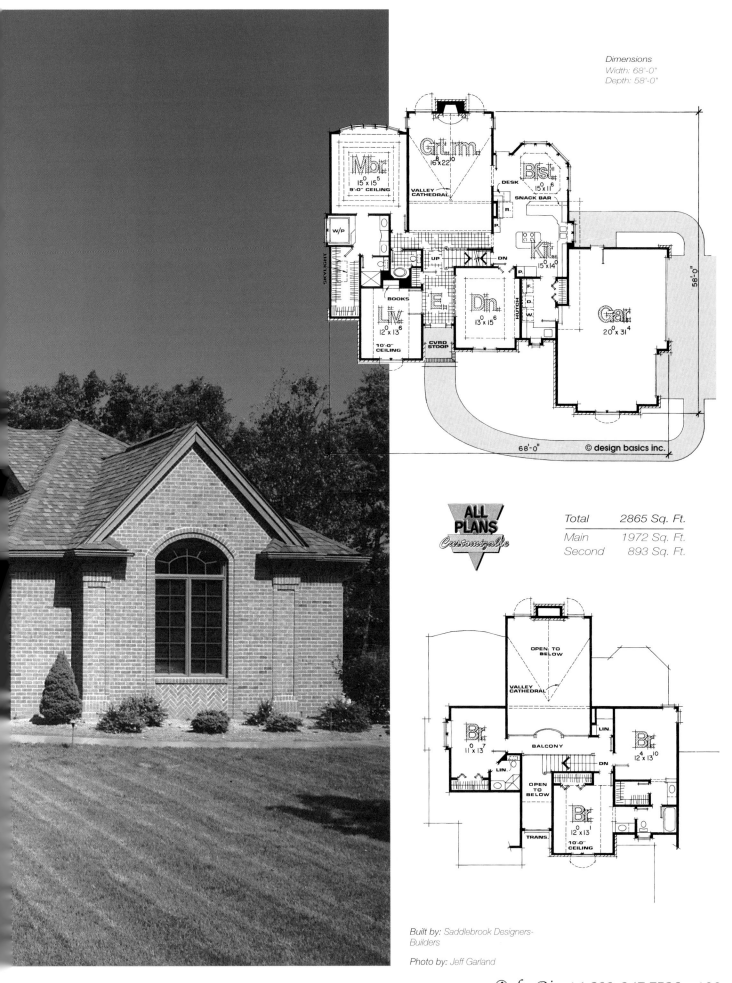

Mbr
15⁰ x 15⁵
9'-0" CEILING

Grt. rm.
16⁸ x 22⁰

Bfst.
15⁰ x 11⁶

DESK

SNACK BAR

VALLEY
CATHEDRAL

Kit.
15⁰ x 14⁰

W/P

SKYLIGHT

UP

DN

Dn.
13⁰ x 15⁶

HUTCH

Gar.
20⁰ x 31⁴

BOOKS

Liv.
12⁰ x 13⁶

E.

10'-0"
CEILING

CVRD
STOOP

© design basics inc.

68'-0"

58'-0"

ALL
PLANS
Customizable

Total	2865 Sq. Ft.
Main	1972 Sq. Ft.
Second	893 Sq. Ft.

OPEN TO
BELOW

VALLEY
CATHEDRAL

Br.
11⁰ x 13⁷

LIN.

BALCONY

LIN.

Br.
12⁴ x 13¹⁰

OPEN
TO
BELOW

DN

Br.
12⁰ x 13¹
10'-0"
CEILING

TRANS.

*Built by: Saddlebrook Designers-
Builders*

Photo by: Jeff Garland

THE MANNING

2207-PC6

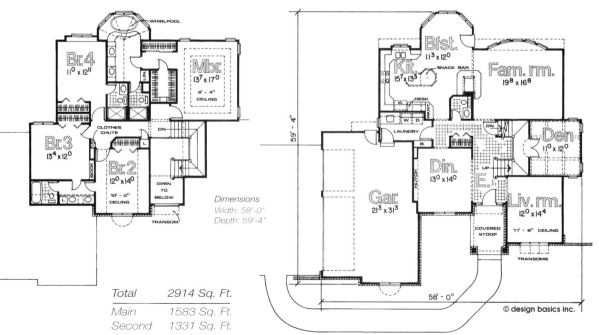

Dimensions
Width: 58'-0"
Depth: 59'-4"

Total	2914 Sq. Ft.
Main	1583 Sq. Ft.
Second	1331 Sq. Ft.

Top Left: An aspect of the kitchen that highlights its expanse.

Top Right: A dining room off the entry that welcomes a view of the living room.

Below Left: An unforgettable skyscape painted on the living room ceiling.

Below Right: The expanded master suite, where a three-sided fireplace was added for atmosphere.

Built by:
Smith Baron Inc.

Photos by:
Roy Engelbrecht

Purple autumn light. A slumbering city and a masterpiece.

Open formal rooms at the entry, embodying a sense of unconstrained elegance.

Sloped ceilings in the master bath. A private mid-level den that gracefully captures attention.

Price Code: 29

This home may have been altered from the plan's original design. For more information on the Manning refer to the index at the back of the book.

THE MANNING 2207-PC6

Above: An invitation to a distinctive den.

Below: Views from the staircase – the mid-level den and lower level, which was opened up to enhance the drama.

Photos by: Roy Engelbrecht

Those You'll Never Forget

They've been there from before the time you could walk, helping you celebrate each milestone in your life.

They were your grandparents, aunts and uncles, or cherished friends of your parents. You most vividly remember them on occasional Sunday mornings when they would come over for coffee. It's amazing that after so many years, the thought of them still has the power to move you.

Photos courtesy of: Scott Silbernick - Top;
Kathy Miller - Middle; Sherri Rydl - Bottom

THE SINCLAIR
1748-PC6

A moment in a day.

A momentary aspect of a ranch home. A clever use of a three-sided fireplace. A secluded bedroom wing. A skylit whirlpool bath. A 12-foot dining room ceiling that speaks its own language.

Price Code: 19   This home may have been altered from the plan's original design. For more information on the Sinclair refer to the index at the back of the book.

Total Square Feet 1911

Dimensions
Width: 56'-0"
Depth: 58'-0"

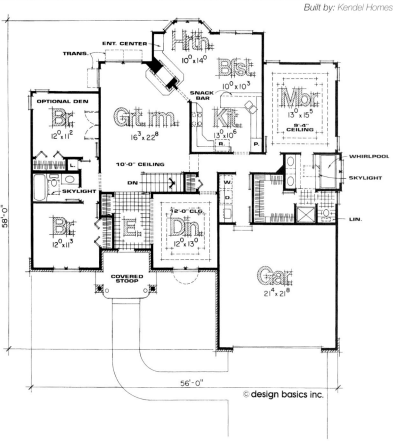

THE BEAUMONT
1388-PC6

A comfortable classic with large windows and a friendly aura.

A breakfast area that gets noticed for its shape. The kitchen with a pleasant surprise — a fireplace. Barrel vault ceiling in the master suite. A sink and iron-a-way — standards in an exceptional laundry room.

Price Code: 22   This home may have been altered from the plan's original design. For more information on the Beaumont refer to the index at the back of the book.

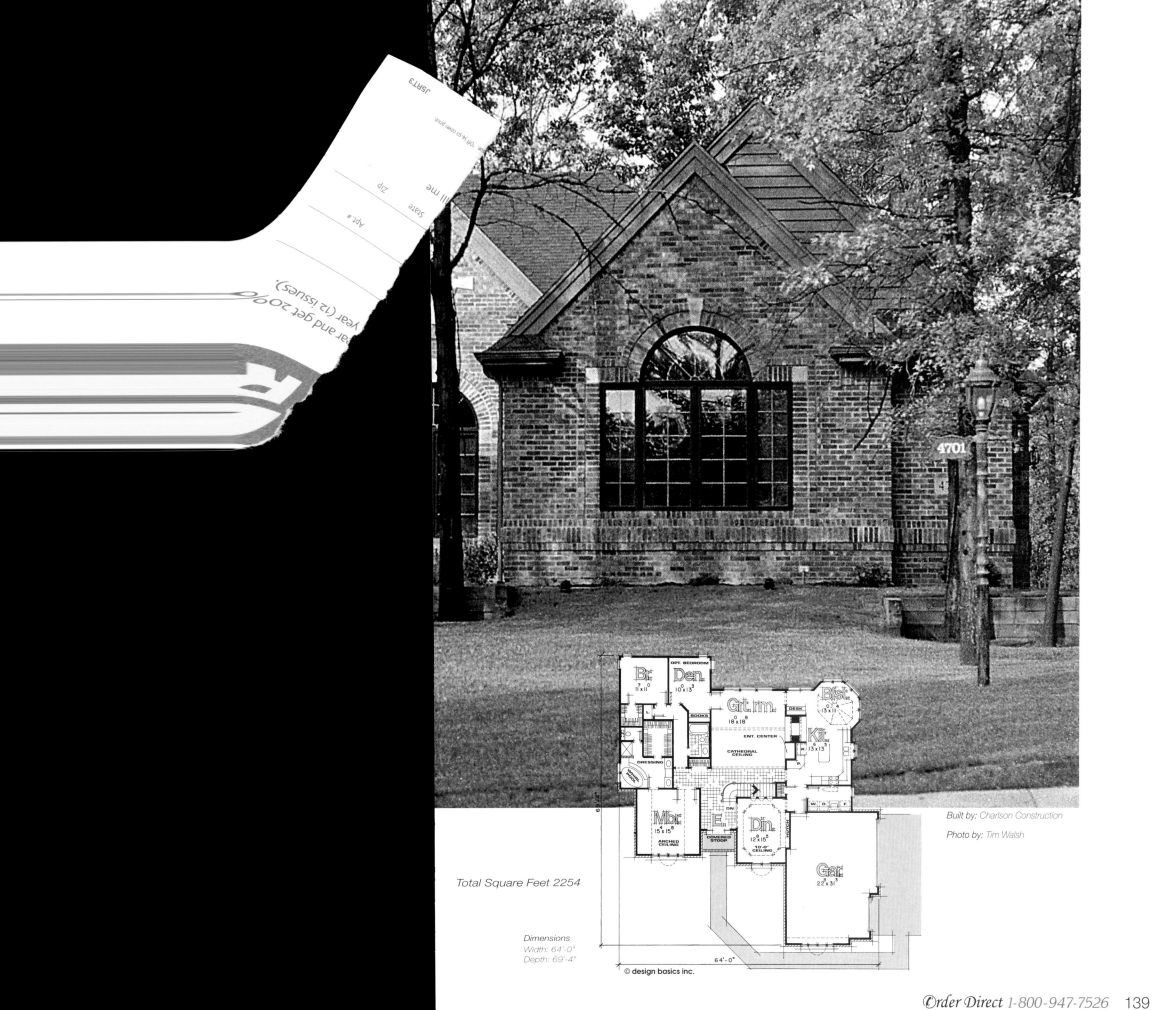

Built by: Charlson Construction

Photo by: Tim Walsh

Total Square Feet 2254

Dimensions
Width: 64'-0"
Depth: 69'-4"

© design basics inc.

THE NORMANDY

2249-PC6

Top Left: Views in the two-story entry: A coat closet. A den with French doors and arched glass.

Bottom Left: A relaxed atmosphere in the great room.

Top Right: The addition of space for twin armoires in the master bedroom.

Bottom Right: The warmth of sunlight on the whirlpool tub.

Built by: Kendel Homes

Interior Photos by: Jeff Bebee

Total	3172 Sq. Ft.
Main	2252 Sq. Ft.
Second	920 Sq. Ft.

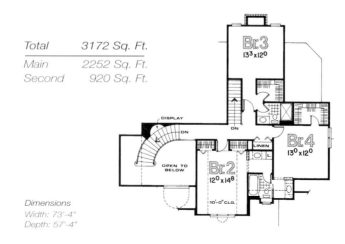

Dimensions
Width: 73'-4"
Depth: 57'-4"

Yesterdays and tomorrows in a bl[...] brick and stucco.

Fluid movement from kitchen to hearth room and beyond.

A 12-foot ceiling in the master bath. Two fireplaces —

just the number to spoil yourself.

Price Code: 31   This home may have been altered from the plan's original design.
For more information about the Normandy refer to the index at the back of the book.

THE NORMANDY 2249-PC6

Top: The organized island kitchen and readily-accessible breakfast area.

Middle: Two chairs and a fire warm the hearth room.

Bottom: A gentle welcome into the dining room.

Interior Photos by: Jeff Bebee

Cousins

You can't quite put your finger on what made them so wonderful. Perhaps it's that they epitomized the closeness of your brothers and sisters, and at the same time all things wonderful about best friends. There were childhood games you

seemed to only play on the occasions you saw them. Games with names like "Black Bear" that somehow became synonymous with your remembrance

of holidays and reunions. The best part of seeing them all again, is the chance to rehash these memories, to laugh at the golden moments, and to once again in unison scream "Black Bear!"

Photos courtesy of: Bruce Arant - Top & Middle; Joni Vazzano- Bottom

THE GREENSBORO

2326-PC6

A hint of lavender in harmony with brick.

A servery convenient to the dining room. The third bedroom, perfect as a guest room.

A partially covered patio for those who favor being out in the open.

Price Code: 21 This home may have been altered from the plan's original design.
For more information about the Greensboro refer to the index at the back of the book.

Built by: Nick's Custom Built Homes

Photos by: Steve Echols Photography

Total Square Feet 2172

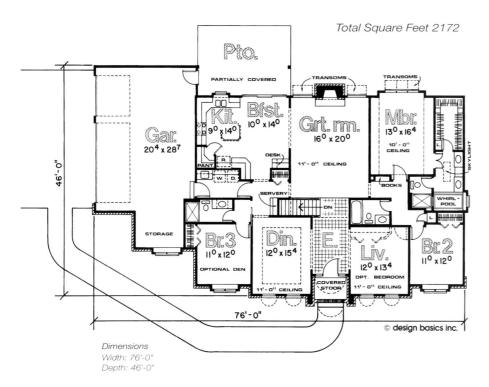

Pto.
PARTIALLY COVERED

TRANSOMS   TRANSOMS

Gar.
20⁴ x 28⁷

Kit.
9⁰ x 14⁰

Bfst.
10⁰ x 14⁰

Grt. rm.
16⁰ x 20⁰
11' - 0" CEILING

Mbr.
13⁰ x 16⁴
10' - 0" CEILING

PANT.

DESK

W. D.

SERVERY

BOOKS

SKYLIGHT

WHIRL-POOL

STORAGE

Br. 3
11⁰ x 12⁰
OPTIONAL DEN

Din.
12⁰ x 15⁴
11' - 0" CEILING

DN

Liv.
12⁰ x 13⁴
OPT. BEDROOM
11' - 0" CEILING

Br. 2
11⁰ x 12⁰

COVERED STOOP

46'-0"

76'-0"

© design basics inc.

Dimensions
Width: 76'-0"
Depth: 46'-0"

Above: Neutral colors in the entry, brightened with a suggestion of sunshine.

THE HARRISON
3174-PC6

Bold. Astute. Understated perfection in exterior details.

Inside, a wide entry with an appeal from the living room. Boxed beams and double doors in the den. Above the garage, a play area perhaps. And an informal area to the rear with room for family and whomever drops by.

Price Code: 34   This home may have been altered from the plan's original design. For more information about the Harrison refer to the index at the back of the book.

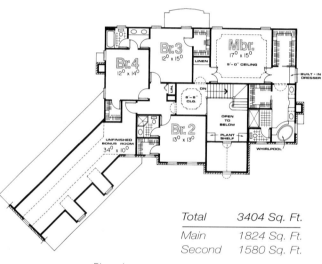

Total	3404 Sq. Ft.
Main	*1824 Sq. Ft.*
Second	*1580 Sq. Ft.*

Dimensions
Width: 83'-4"
Depth: 67'-10"

Built by: Bob Lucente Construction

Built by:
*Saddlebrook
Designers-Builders*

Photo by:
Jeff Garland

Bfst.
15⁰ x 11⁸
9' - 0"
CLG.

Grt. rm.
15¹⁰ x 21¹⁰

Mbr.
13⁰ x 16⁸
10' - 0"
CLG.

WET BAR

SKYLIGHT

SNACK BAR

DESK

BOOKS

Kit.
15⁰ x 14³

DN

UP

SHELVES

Din.
12⁸ x 15²

HUTCH

Liv.
11⁴ x 14⁵
10' - 0"
CEILING

Gar.
30⁸ x 21⁰

W. D.

P.

CVRD.
STOOP

OPEN TO
GREAT ROOM

SKYLIGHT

Br. 2
12⁸ x 11⁶

PLANT SHELF

Br. 4
12⁰ x 13⁶

DN

OPEN
TO
BELOW

Br. 3
11⁸ x 13⁰

TRANS.

51' - 3"

66' - 0"

© design basics inc.

Dimensions
Width: 66'-0"
Depth: 51'-3"

Total   2582 Sq. Ft.
Main   1748 Sq. Ft.
Second   834 Sq. Ft.

THE LAFAYETTE

829-PC6

The feel of a country cottage and a refreshing breeze.

Open skylit great room. Great communication between kitchen and breakfast area. Features here include: a lengthy snack bar counter, wet bar, work desk and bayed windows.

Price Code: 25   This home may have been altered from the plan's original design.
For more information on the Lafayette refer to the index at the back of the book.

That Someone Special

*It seems that all your life
you'd been searching for each other.
And when you finally met
it was better than all the Valentines Day
cards ever said it could be.
Millions have futilely tried to describe
what perhaps can never be defined.
It is a union that neither miles
nor wars could ever sever.
And as one of the lucky ones,
you've found it.*

Photos courtesy of: Bruce Arant - Top; Alva Louden - Bottom

THE ALBANY

2235-PC6

Evening hues on a home where the light was left on for you.

Tradition in the front porch. Formality in the dining room off the entry.

Yet, a bit of ease in the sunniness of the great room and breakfast area.

Price Code: 19

This home may have been altered from the plan's original design. For more information on the Albany refer to the index at the back of the book.

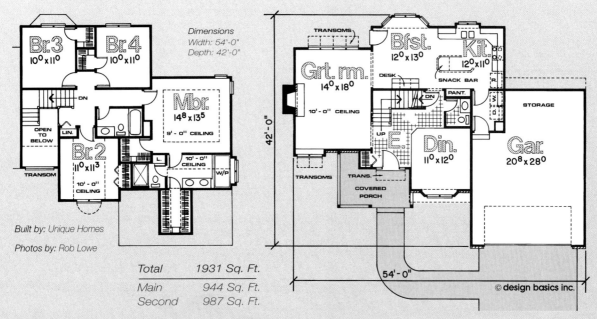

Dimensions
Width: 54'-0"
Depth: 42'-0"

Br. 3 10⁰ x 11⁰
Br. 4 10⁰ x 11⁰
Mbr. 14⁸ x 13⁵ 9'-0" CEILING
Br. 2 11⁰ x 11³ 10'-0" CEILING

Bfst. 12⁰ x 13⁰
Kit. 12⁰ x 11⁰
Grt. rm. 14⁰ x 18⁰ 10'-0" CEILING
Din. 11⁰ x 12⁰
Gar. 20⁸ x 28⁰
STORAGE

Built by: Unique Homes

Photos by: Rob Lowe

Total	1931 Sq. Ft.
Main	944 Sq. Ft.
Second	987 Sq. Ft.

© design basics inc.

THE ROTHSCHILD

2374-PC6

Built by: Oehlberg Construction

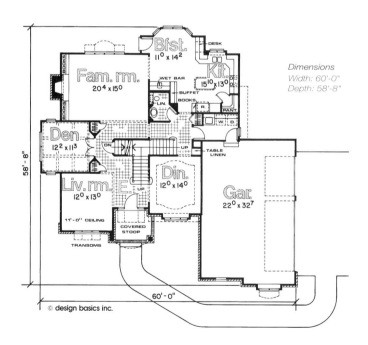

Dimensions
Width: 60'-0"
Depth: 58'-8"

Fam. rm. 20⁴ x 15⁰
Bfst. 11⁰ x 14²
Kit. 15¹⁰ x 13⁰
Den 12² x 11³
Liv. rm. 12⁰ x 13⁰
Din. 12⁰ x 14⁰
Gar. 22⁰ x 32⁷
11'-0" CEILING
58'-8"
60'-0"
© design basics inc.

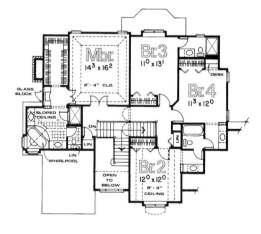

Mbr. 14³ x 16²
Br. 3 11⁰ x 13¹
Br. 4 11³ x 12⁰
Br. 2 12⁰ x 12⁰
9'-4" CEILING
OPEN TO BELOW
WHIRLPOOL

ALL PLANS
Customizable

Total	2870 Sq. Ft.
Main	1575 Sq. Ft.
Second	1295 Sq. Ft.

Amid a distant array of clouds, a finished demeanor.

A T-shaped stairway for two ways up and down. An entertaining kitchen with buffet, wet bar and walk-in pantry. A bit of pampering in the bedrooms — three with their own vanity and the master with separate make-up counter.

Price Code: 28   This home may have been altered from the plan's original design. For more information on the Rothschild refer to the index at the back of the book.

COMING HOME ᔓ

Photo courtesy of: Rita Hamele

You wish you were there. Where their grins, their sticky-lollipopped fingers, their stout, overalled shoulders would make a place for you on their front porch. They are bonded by a tie known as family. Together at a place called home.

HOME PLAN INDEX

THE ORIGINAL DESIGNS OF SOME OF THE HOMES FEATURED in this book were altered when built. To give you a better understanding of our home plans, the following pages provide artists' renderings of each home's originally-designed front elevation, as well as a few points of interest describing the design.

AS YOU STUDY THESE DESIGNS, KEEP IN MIND that all Design Basics home plans can be customized according to your needs by our Custom Change department. More information about Design Basics Custom Changes can be found on page 161.

IF YOU DESIRE ADDITIONAL INFORMATION regarding any of these home plan designs, or about custom changes, call a Design Basics Customer Support Specialist at (800) 947-7526, Monday - Friday, 7:00 a.m. - 6:00 p.m. C.T.

3

THE KELSEY
3019-PC6

- 1479 *square feet*
- *the master bedroom features a 9'high ceiling*
- *the enclosed laundry room has a window*
- *the volume great room displays tall windows*
- *the den can convert to another bedroom*

THE ARMBURST
2723-PC6

- 2645 *square feet*
- *the entry's view centers on the great room's 3 windows*
- *a planning desk is beneficial in the dinette*
- *the kitchen area offers spaciousness to eat and entertain*
- *double doors open into the pampering master bedroom*

4

6

THE LANCASTER
1752-PC6

• 1846 *square feet*
• *the 2-story entry has a large coat closet and plant shelf*
• *unloading groceries is easy from garage to kitchen*
• *an arched window lights a secondary bedroom*
• *the dining room has a lovely view to the front*

7

THE BANCROFT
1559-PC6

• 1808 *square feet*
• *bayed windows brighten the volume great room*
• *the master bedroom has a 10' high ceiling*
• *two comfortable bedrooms share a compartmented bath*
• *abundant counter space optimizes the kitchen*

8

THE EDMONTON
2309-PC6

• 2579 *square feet*
• *a tiered ceiling highlights the dinette*
• *a walk-in pantry equips the kitchen*
• *the kitchen, hearth room and breakfast area are spacious*
• *the dining room is visible from the entry*

11

THE MEDINAH MANOR
9147-PC6

• 3677 *square feet*
• *his and her walk-in closets highlight the master suite*
• *a see-thru fireplace connects the living and family rooms*
• *the large kitchen features an island cooktop*
• *a covered rear porch is accessed through the mud room*

12

THE INGRAM
2281-PC6

• 1778 *square feet*
• *the elevation displays an inviting front porch*
• *the bayed dining room includes space for a hutch*
• *two second-floor bedrooms share a full bath*
• *a tiered ceiling adds intrigue to the master bedroom*

13

THE ADAIR
2300-PC6

• 1496 *square feet*
• *the dining room's location enhances family gatherings*
• *windows and a fireplace entice the great room*
• *boxed windows bring character to the front rooms*
• *the master suite enjoys a sunlit whirlpool tub*

14

THE CRAWFORD
2408-PC6

• 2270 *square feet*
• *the great room and hearth room share a see-thru fireplace*
• *the sunny breakfast area has direct access to the back*
• *a large linen closet serves upstairs bedrooms*
• *the formal dining room offers space for a hutch*

16

THE ORCHARD
2818-PC6

• 1651 *square feet*
• *the laundry room offers a soaking sink*
• *wrapping counters equip the kitchen*
• *bedroom #2 features a 10' high ceiling*
• *a wet bar services the entertaining den*

17

THE DOVER
2376-PC6

• 1205 *square feet*
• *the kitchen reveals a large snack bar*
• *the great room enjoys a window-flanked fireplace*
• *the secondary bedroom offers privacy to guests*
• *the master suite boasts a roomy walk-in closet*

18

THE FAYETTE
2346-PC6

• 2480 *square feet*
• *the 16-foot-high entry showcases an above balcony*
• *French doors open into the den with built-in bookshelves*
• *an island kitchen is open to the bayed dinette*
• *a tiered ceiling adds interest to the master bedroom*

151

19

THE TANNER
3249-PC6

- 2282 square feet
- an organized kitchen boasts a central island counter
- an arched window adds individuality to bedroom #2
- prominent windows flood light into the great room
- a large laundry room provides a sink and window

20

THE CHURCHILL
2016-PC6

- 3950 square feet
- a wet bar is located in the formal living room
- a large gathering room adjoins the kitchen/breakfast area
- a family staircase eases traffic from the back of the home
- a spider-beamed ceiling decorates the den

22

THE ELDRIDGE
3064-PC6

- 2055 square feet
- the kitchen is organized with an island counter
- the laundry room has the benefit of a soaking sink
- windows view the front and back in the great room
- a dual-lav bath serves the 3 upstairs bedrooms

23

THE HARRISBURG
2315-PC6

- 1993 square feet
- French doors connect the living room and family room
- the family room is open to the breakfast area and kitchen
- the laundry room serves as a mud entry
- the master suite has a 10-foot-high ceiling and luxury bath

24

THE EDGEWOOD
2839-PC6

- 3057 square feet
- a window seat adds warmth to bedroom #2
- bayed windows bring character to the den
- the sunny kitchen/breakfast area is open to the family room
- the indulging master suite offers many luxurious amenities

25

THE PARNELL
3089-PC6

- 1712 square feet
- the sunny great room features abundant windows
- a plant shelf decorates the two-story entry
- the spacious laundry room offers a soaking sink
- double doors further seclude the master suite

26

THE CANTERBURY
2411-PC6

- 3623 square feet
- a large courtyard adds intrigue to the front elevation
- a sweeping staircase and open views grace the high entry
- the bayed dinette brightens the kitchen area
- cozy fireplaces warm the great and hearth rooms

29

THE LINDEN
2638-PC6

- 2103 square feet
- handsome bookcases frame the family room's fireplace
- double doors open into the family room for added privacy
- the kitchen has convenient access to the laundry area
- the formal parlor provides a second living area

30

THE STRATMAN
3588-PC6

- 2198 square feet
- the casual family room includes a fireplace
- the dining room leads to the kitchen through French doors
- an upstairs balcony overlooks the entry below
- the master suite has abundant room for expansion

31

THE LOGAN
1551-PC6

- 1271 square feet
- a cathedral ceiling adds spaciousness to the great room
- the efficient kitchen is strategically near the garage
- a full bath serves two secondary bedrooms
- the laundry room is located near the bedrooms

32

The Pinnacle
3284-PC6

- 2496 square feet
- the entry views both the dining room and the den
- the great room has a 2-story ceiling and fireplace
- the peninsula kitchen offers a snack bar, desk and pantry
- bayed windows add drama in the master bedroom

34

The Ambrose
2701-PC6

- 2340 square feet
- a skylit vanity highlights the master bath
- the formal dining room features hutch space
- three second-floor bedrooms share a dual-lav bath
- the sunny breakfast area has access to the back

35

The Ashville
2811-PC6

- 2277 square feet
- a large vanity complements the master bath
- French doors add a formal touch to the dinette
- the two-story entry includes a plant shelf
- a spacious corridor organizes the upstairs bedrooms

36

The Cyprus
2648-PC6

- 1951 square feet
- French doors open to the formal parlor
- an island kitchen offers a large pantry and desk
- the laundry room serves as a mud entry
- a window seat warms the master bedroom

37

The Arant
2261-PC6

- 2405 square feet
- tall windows dominate the great room
- the laundry room features a sink and access outdoors
- the master bedroom is decorated with corner windows
- the powder bath is centrally located on the main floor

The Lawrence
2652-PC6

- 2512 square feet
- twin curio cabinets benefit the den
- the hearth kitchen features an island cooktop
- twin columns dignify the dining room
- a see-thru fireplace warms the great room

38

40

The Quimby
3010-PC6

- 1422 square feet
- a 12' high ceiling connects the kitchen and great room
- extra storage and a work bench benefit the garage
- windows on two walls bring light to the dinette
- bedroom #3 has the option of converting to a den

The Ashworth
3103-PC6

- 1700 square feet
- a snack bar serves the bright dinette
- a U-shaped stairway leads to the second floor
- a dual-lav bath serves the secondary bedrooms
- a 9' high ceiling adds space to the master bedroom

41

The Fraser
2173-PC6

- 1451 square feet
- a snack bar services the breakfast area
- the pleasant dinette offers access to the rear
- the master suite boasts a 9' high boxed ceiling
- a 10' high ceiling joins the entry and great room

42

The Paige
3581-PC6

- 1771 square feet
- the formal dining room is flexible as a parlor
- patio doors lead to the back from the breakfast area
- the L-shaped porch has room for a swing
- the family room has a beautiful view to the back

43

44

THE FAIRCHILD
2733-PC6

- 3904 *square feet*
- *the den is highlighted with a lovely window*
- *the living room offers dramatic views of the covered porch*
- *the family room is situated for privacy on the main floor*
- 3 *upstairs bedrooms feature walk-in closets*

47

THE HARTFORD
2458-PC6

- 2932 *square feet*
- *the entry offers vistas past the great room and veranda*
- *the den, with fireplace, is accessed by the master bedroom*
- *an island counter organizes the kitchen*
- *sloped ceilings accent the master bath*

48

THE COMSTOCK
2778-PC6

- 2456 *square feet*
- *bedroom #3 has the option of becoming a den*
- *the gathering room functions as a casual eating area*
- *the master suite displays three pairs of French doors*
- *the island kitchen features an entertainment center*

THE SWEETWATER BEND
9119-PC6

49

- 4228 *square feet*
- *the media room is convenient to the kitchen and a wet bar*
- *the sunny dinette enjoys an impressive view*
- *a secluded study is accessible from the master bedroom*
- *secondary bedrooms enjoy significant separation*

50

THE LAVERTON
2248-PC6

- 1650 *square feet*
- *the volume entry is highlighted by a plant ledge*
- *the dinette features a planning desk*
- *bedroom #3 has an arched window*
- *the pampering master suite has abundant closet space*

THE HAWTHORNE
2799-PC6

52

- 1887 *square feet*
- *a laundry room offers access from the garage*
- *the kitchen has the character of a sloped ceiling*
- *openness adds elegance to the dining room*
- *cedar chest highlights a pampering master suite*

53

THE PAISLEY
2618-PC6

- 2131 *square feet*
- *French doors connect the living room and family room*
- *the elegant dining room includes a built-in curio cabinet*
- *a handy laundry area adjoins storage space in the garage*
- *the master bath has pampering amenities of larger homes*

THE MANSFIELD
1539-PC6

54

- 1996 *square feet*
- *the organized kitchen boasts a snack bar and desk*
- *bookshelves are featured in the volume great room*
- *the breakfast area enjoys tall windows*
- *the dining room has an 11' high ceiling*

55

THE TYNDALE
2245-PC6

- 1685 *square feet*
- *a volume ceiling brings spaciousness to the great room*
- *an elegant boxed window shines in the dining room*
- *a desk and snack bar serve the breakfast area*
- *two linen closets serve the secondary bedrooms*

THE SHAWNEE
2461-PC6

56

- 1850 *square feet*
- *tall windows add brightness throughout the home*
- *a porch extends the living area of the home*
- *the island kitchen offers a desk*
- *a large corridor secludes the bedroom wing*

THE PINEHURST
2311-PC6

- 2486 square feet
- the den features French doors and a volume ceiling
- the secluded family area has an island kitchen
- an open, curving stairway views the living room
- unfinished storage potential exists on the second floor

THE BRIARWOOD
2956-PC6

- 2562 square feet
- the dining room has a lovely view to the front
- tall windows add space to the master bedroom
- a large utility area connects the kitchen and garage
- the master suite enjoys an arched, private entrance

THE BARRINGTON WOOD
1035-PC6

- 2967 square feet
- the entry views a magnificent curved stairway
- two secondary bedrooms have walk-in closets
- French doors access the den with a built-in bookcase
- columns frame the entrance into the great room

THE AURORA
2836-PC6

- 2308 square feet
- bookshelves give personality to the master suite
- tall, bowed windows compliment the great room
- a double vanity serves 3 upstairs bedrooms
- a wet bar is convenient to the formal dining room

THE NEWBERRY
1455-PC6

- 2594 square feet
- a bayed whirlpool tub entices the master suite
- French doors connect the living and dining rooms
- the kitchen is open to a breakfast area and sunroom
- his and her vanities serve 3 upstairs bedrooms

THE KAPLIN
1963-PC6

- 1347 square feet
- a snack bar and pantry organize the kitchen
- a 10' high ceiling creates space in the entry
- bedroom #3 has the option of becoming a den
- windows flank the fireplace in the great room

THE KINGSBURY
2445-PC6

- 2814 square feet
- the entry provides first impressions of spaciousness
- tall, arched windows brighten the great room
- the master suite is well-separated for privacy
- French doors connect the living and family rooms

THE MONTROSE
2127-PC6

- 2256 square feet
- the dining room is brightened by a window
- bayed windows are located in bedroom #2
- the family room features an entertainment center
- a skylight brightens the master bath vanity

THE CIMMERON
2215-PC6

- 2854 square feet
- grocery traffic is simplified from the garage to the kitchen
- extra counter space helps serve the dining room
- the staircase landing is brightened by an arched window
- the master suite includes a variety of luxurious amenities

THE BERMIER
2236-PC6

- 1855 square feet
- a boxed window brightens the dining room
- wrapping counters organize the kitchen
- bedroom #4 features a 10' high ceiling
- a powder bath is centrally located

73

THE SANTA ANA
987-PC6
- 3025 square feet
- bedroom #3 has a 10' high ceiling
- the library has French doors and three bookcases
- the hearth room includes an entertainment center
- a 2-person whirlpool tub is in the master bath

74

THE LE GRAND
2218-PC6
- 3689 square feet
- windows with transoms highlight the living room
- an informal back staircase is perfect for the family
- a 4-car garage provides extra storage space
- the bayed dinette features unique ceiling detail

77

THE RENWICK
2230-PC6
- 2957 square feet
- trapezoid windows illuminate the great room
- the dining room's French doors lead to the nearby kitchen
- a large utility room is located near the garage
- an oval whirlpool tub pampers the master bath

78

THE FRANKLIN
2316-PC6
- 2345 square feet
- the elevation reflects a true American Colonial
- the family room boasts bayed windows
- bedroom #2 features its own bath
- a streamlined path joins the dining room and kitchen

79

THE STANTON
2414-PC6
- 2343 square feet
- sloped ceilings characterize the master bath
- boxed windows brighten bedrooms #3 and #4
- the open breakfast area is served by a snack bar
- secondary bedrooms are served by a walk-in linen closet

80

THE HAZELTON
1019-PC6
- 2219 square feet
- the covered porch is perfect for relaxing
- a skylight brightens the master suite vanity
- the master suite greets you at the top of the stairs
- the secondary bedrooms share a dual-lav bath

83

THE ELDORADO
2719-PC6
- 1976 square feet
- a volume ceiling highlights the master bedroom
- the garage has the benefit of a storage area
- an island offers daily cooking ease in the kitchen
- the second-floor bedrooms share a double vanity bath

84

THE PRAIRIE
2285-PC6
- 2115 square feet
- the 2-story entry surveys two large living areas
- the great room showcases trapezoid windows
- all secondary bedrooms are secluded upstairs
- bedroom #4 features a volume ceiling

85

THE BALDWIN
2962-PC6
- 2377 square feet
- a streamlined path joins the kitchen and dining room
- the media room offers versatility for informal gatherings
- bayed windows light up the dinette and family room
- the master suite enjoys privacy and a secluded entrance

86

THE CORDEAUX
2174-PC6
- 2708 square feet
- entertainment shelves benefit the family room
- a bayed whirlpool tub highlights the master bath
- bedroom #4 features its own ¾ bath
- a 3-car garage offers room for another vehicle

89

THE NEWMAN
1689-PC6

- 2133 square feet
- diagonal views inside provide an expansive feel
- the kitchen and dinette offer lovely windows
- the master suite features a sunny whirlpool tub
- extra storage is a benefit to the 3-car garage

THE BRISTOL
1870-PC6

- 2078 square feet
- gingerbread and arches highlight the elevation
- bayed windows illuminate bedroom #2
- the sunken gathering room is warmed by a fireplace
- the bayed breakfast area is open to the kitchen

90

92

THE BRENNAN
3493-PC6

- 2745 square feet
- a wrought iron railing compliments the front porch
- a plant shelf decorates the 2-story entry
- the kitchen is open to a sunny gazebo breakfast area
- a beamed ceiling adds character to the living room

THE STERLING
1540-PC6

- 2727 square feet
- built-in bookshelves benefit a secondary bedroom
- a T-shaped staircase accesses the second level
- the laundry room features a soaking sink
- upstairs, double doors lead to the master bedroom

94

96

THE LEIGHTON
2377-PC6

- 1636 square feet
- a barrel-vaulted porch highlights the elevation
- the great room has a fireplace flanked by windows
- the dining room is conveniently near the kitchen
- a work bench organizes storage in the garage

THE SIERRA
2745-PC6

- 2089 square feet
- a large pantry benefits the kitchen
- the garage has extra space for a work bench
- tall, bayed windows illuminate the breakfast area
- a 3-sided fireplace opens to the great room

97

98

THE MEADOWVIEW MANOR
9114-PC6

- 4139 square feet
- massive windows dominate the 2-story living room
- the kitchen/breakfast area opens to a covered rear porch
- bayed windows brighten the dining room
- built-in shelves benefit the family room

THE MANCHESTER
1862-PC6

- 2353 square feet
- a clothes chute benefits the second-floor bedrooms
- secondary bedrooms share a compartmented bath
- the master bedroom features a volume ceiling
- the kitchen is equipped with a walk-in pantry

101

102

THE WRENWOOD
3005-PC6

- 2186 square feet
- the kitchen displays an island cooktop
- bedroom #3 boasts a 10' high ceiling
- bright windows decorate the great room
- a sloped ceiling adds excitement to the master bath

THE MONTE VISTA
1032-PC6

- 1697 square feet
- an arched window decorates the volume dining room
- windows with transoms enhance the great room
- a 10' high ceiling dramatizes the master bedroom
- grocery traffic is streamlined from garage to kitchen

103

104

THE CARLTON
1588-PC6

- 3473 square feet
- stately columns flank the covered stoop
- strategic placement secludes secondary bedrooms
- a laundry room features iron-a-away and sink
- the formal rooms provide an area to entertain

THE MEREDITH
2312-PC6

- 2113 square feet
- a sloped ceiling adds drama in the sunken family room
- a walk-in linen closet serves the secondary bedrooms
- tall windows add elegance to the living room
- a snack bar and two lazy Susans equip the kitchen

106

THE LARAMY
3555-PC6

- 1518 square feet
- a desk aids the breakfast area
- a 9' high ceiling adorns bedroom #2
- a generous walk-in closet serves the master suite
- the laundry room features a soaking sink

107

THE SAN BERNARD
940-PC6

- 3038 square feet
- a 2-story entry boasts coat closets with plant shelves
- a built-in window seat in one secondary bedroom
- a wet bar is accessible to the sunken great room
- the U-shaped stairway leads to three bedrooms

108

THE COLLIER
2216-PC6

- 2174 square feet
- the living and dining rooms are open to one another
- the large master suite has a 9' high ceiling
- the laundry room offers a soaking sink
- both upstairs bath areas are brightened by skylights

111

THE CHANDLER
1554-PC6

- 2276 square feet
- a large bath serves the upstairs bedrooms
- the 2-story entry opens to the formal dining room
- a fireplace and 10'5" ceiling grace the great room
- the island kitchen has a pantry and a built-in desk

112

THE HANNIBAL
898-PC6

- 2360 square feet
- the family room features bookshelves and a fireplace
- the island kitchen greets the open dinette
- a discrete main floor powder bath is conveniently located
- the master bedroom features a vaulted ceiling

113

THE HAWKESBURY
2206-PC6

- 2498 square feet
- bedroom #3 can be a private sitting room
- a gazebo dinette is open to the family room
- the kitchen has an island cooktop and snack bar
- the family room features entertainment shelving

114

THE ASHTON
2203-PC6

- 2391 square feet
- a 2-sided fireplace warms the great room
- tall windows brighten the master suite whirlpool
- bayed windows and a desk optimize the dinette
- the living room features a dramatic high ceiling

117

THE KENDALL
1553-PC6

- 2387 square feet
- bayed windows and a desk optimize the dinette
- a large laundry room has space for a freezer
- extra space is provided in the garage for storage
- interesting angles add design character to the bedrooms

118

119

THE MONTEREY
2290-PC6

- 1666 square feet
- the entry invites with a bright arched transom
- the dining room displays a lovely window
- the secluded master bedroom enjoys a vaulted ceiling
- two secondary bedrooms share a convenient bath

THE DUNDEE
2476-PC6

- 2884 square feet
- the entry surveys the dining room and great room
- the great room features a large bowed window
- the den is accessed from the master suite
- a walk-in cedar closet is located upstairs

120

THE ROSEBURY
1767-PC6

- 1604 square feet
- two secondary bedrooms share a full bath
- the dining room is highlighted by a formal ceiling
- the kitchen includes a window box above the sink
- an expansive great room is visible from the entry

THE PATERSON
1380-PC6

- 1999 square feet
- guests are welcomed on an inviting front porch
- a walk-in pantry organizes the kitchen
- space above the garage can be finished for storage
- the master suite includes a sloped ceiling

122

124

THE EASTGATE
2406-PC6

- 3827 square feet
- a gallery wall in the entry adds impact to first impressions
- a 12' high ceiling adds volume to the den
- the master suite adjoins a private covered veranda
- spacious upstairs bedrooms enjoy private walk-in closets

THE ABBEY
1510-PC6

- 3306 square feet
- the kitchen has a salad sink and island snack bar
- a T-shaped stairway organizes traffic in living areas
- two walk-in closets benefit the master bedroom
- a private ¾ bath is convenient for the guest bedroom

126

128

THE BARTELS
2579-PC6

- 1594 square feet
- the living and dining rooms join for expanded entertaining
- French doors enclose the dining room
- the kitchen offers a large pantry and snack bar
- the laundry room offers a sink

THE NEWPORT
2293-PC6

- 2890 square feet
- a bayed window and bookcase highlight the den
- the comfortable family room displays a fireplace
- a second walk-in closet adds space to the master suite
- the dining room is strategically near the kitchen

130

131

THE REMINGTON
1486-PC6

- 2865 square feet
- a large transom window brightens the 2-story entry
- the great room dramatizes a valley cathedral ceiling
- a skylight lights up the master suite's closet
- generous baths accommodate second-floor bedrooms

THE MANNING
2207-PC6

- 2914 square feet
- the family room shares a 3-sided fireplace
- bedroom #4 boasts its own bath
- the bayed dinette enjoys a view of the fireplace
- the master suite features two generous closets

132

134

159

137

138

THE SINCLAIR
1748-PC6

- 1911 square feet
- wrapping counter space benefits the kitchen
- the hearth room provides a comfortable place to relax
- a corner sink and snack bar highlight the kitchen
- a large walk-in closet completes the master bath

THE BEAUMONT
1388-PC6

- 2254 square feet
- floor-to-ceiling windows brighten the great room
- the master bath includes glass block in the shower
- a private den has double doors to the great room
- a walk-in closet benefits the second bedroom

140

143

THE NORMANDY
2249-PC6

- 3172 square feet
- arched windows offer views out the great room
- the master bedroom features a private back door
- the hearth room's fireplace opens to the dinette
- French doors reveal the den with built-in bookcase

THE GREENSBORO
2326-PC6

- 2172 square feet
- the formal rooms enhance options for entertaining
- picturesque windows frame the great room's fireplace
- a walk-in pantry highlights the island kitchen
- the master bath enjoys a skylit dressing area

144

146

THE HARRISON
3174-PC6

- 3404 square feet
- an island cooktop organizes the kitchen
- the dining room's French doors lead directly to the kitchen
- all secondary bedrooms have immediate access to a bath
- storage space is a benefit in the 3-car garage

THE LAFAYETTE
829-PC6

- 2582 square feet
- the master bedroom enjoys privacy on the main floor
- a powder bath is centrally located
- the master bath boasts a sunny whirlpool tub
- the living room features private French doors

148

149

THE ALBANY
2235-PC6

- 1931 square feet
- the great room is graced with a 10-foot ceiling
- the upstairs landing overlooks the entry below
- an island counter and pantry benefit the kitchen
- the master suite boasts a dressing area and whirlpool

THE ROTHSCHILD
2374-PC6

- 2870 square feet
- the formal rooms enhance the impact of the stunning entry
- French doors reveal the den with 3 windows
- the expansive family room is private from the formal areas
- the master suite's French doors open to a view of the entry

HAVE YOU FOUND A HOME PLAN THAT WOULD BE *PERFECT,*

IF ONLY...

the kitchen was larger?

the garage was a three-car?

the laundry room could be moved?

Let Design Basics custom plan change specialists turn that "almost perfect" home plan into the home of your dreams. Our in-house designers are intimately familiar with each plan, so you can be assured design integrity will be maintained regardless of the change. In addition, our highly-detailed, multiple review process ensures accurate execution of each Design Basics plan change.

You're just a phone call away from the perfect home plan.

For information on changes not listed, or for additional custom plan change consultation at *no additional charge,* call one of our Customer Support Specialist toll-free at

800-947-7526

Mon. - Fri. 7:00 am - 6:00 pm. CT.

CUSTOM CHANGE PRICES

2 X 6 EXTERIOR WALLS .... $150 .....
    FROM STANDARD 2 X 4 TO 2 X 6 EXTERIOR WALLS

EACH GARAGE ALTERATION .... $275 .....
- FRONT-ENTRY TO SIDE LOAD (OR VICE VERSA)
- 2-CAR TO 3-CAR (OR VICE VERSA)
- 2-CAR FRONT-ENTRY TO 3-CAR SIDE -LOAD (OR VICE VERSA)
- 3-CAR FRONT-ENTRY TO 2-CAR SIDE -LOAD (OR VICE VERSA)

WALK-OUT BASEMENT .... $175 .....

CRAWL SPACE FOUNDATION .... $225 .....

SLAB FOUNDATION .... $225 .....

STRETCH CHANGES .... $5 per lineal foot of cut

ADDITIONAL BRICK TO SIDES & REAR .... $325 .....

ADDITIONAL BRICK TO FRONT,
    SIDES AND REAR .... $425 .....

ALTERNATE PRELIMINARY ELEVATION .... $150 .....

9-FOOT MAIN LEVEL WALLS .... starting at $150

SPECIFY WINDOW BRAND .... $95 .....

POURED CONCRETE FOUNDATION .... $25 .....
    ONLY WITH OTHER CHANGES

ADDING ONE COURSE (8") TO THE FOUNDATION HEIGHT
    ONLY WITH OTHER CHANGES .... $25 .....

NOTE ....
- All plan changes come to you on erasable, reproducible vellums.
- An unchanged set of original vellums is available for only $50 along with your plan changes.
- Gold Seal™ changes are not made to the artist's renderings, electrical, sections or cabinets.
- Prices are subject to change.

CALL US WITH ANY QUESTIONS YOU MAY HAVE OR TO SCHEDULE ANY CHANGES NOT LISTED.

DO the right thing with our home plans.

If you've ever paid to have a home plan designed from scratch, you know it's expensive – and time consuming. At Design Basics, we invest thousands of dollars and a vast amount of time to painstakingly develop each one of our home plans. But because of our plan service approach, we can offer our award-winning designs for only a fraction of the cost.

WHAT'S the RIGHT thing?

Each of our home plans have been registered with the U.S. Copyright Office. Because they're copyrighted, you need to be aware of the following points regarding their proper use.

* If you make modifications to a Design Basics home plan, including the artist's rendering of that home plan, the rights to use of the modified plan and the right to claim of copyright in the modified plan are still governed by Design Basics as owner of the copyright of the original home plan.

    NOTE– regardless of how extensive the changes are, no claim to copyright may be made in any modified Design Basics home plan.

* Redrawing and/or constructing a home that utilizes design elements, either in whole or in part, based on a copyrighted Design Basics home plan, constitutes infringement of U.S. copyright law and can carry penalties of up to $100,000 per violation.

WITH this in mind, please respect our COPYRIGHTS !

It's not just the right thing to do... it's the law.

PLANS TO BUILD?

1. Gold Seal™ Home Plan Book Set. 442 of today's most sought-after one-story, 1½ and 2-story home plan ideas.

Book #900P
$19.95 each. SPECIAL OFFER –
Order the set of 5 for $84.95.

> Homes of Distinction – 86 plans under 1800´
> Homes of Sophistication – 106 plans, 1800´ - 2199´
> Homes of Elegance – 107 plans, 2200´ - 2599´
> Homes of Prominence – 75 plans, 2600´ - 2999´
> Homes of Grandeur – 68 plans, 3000´ - 4000´

2. Timeless Legacy™, A Collection of Fine Home Designs by Carmichael & Dame. 52 breathtaking luxury home designs from 3300' to 4500'. Includes artful rear views of each home.

Book #9005P
Available for $25. A leather hardbound, limited edition is also available for $50.

3. Heartland Home Plans™. 120 plan ideas designed for every-day practicality. Warm, unpretentious elevations easily adapt to individual lifestyles.

Book #8005P   *Just $8.95*

4. The Narrow Book™. 217 one-story, 1½ story and 2-story home plans that are from 26 to 50 feet wide. Many can be joined together to create customized duplex plans.

Book #7296P   *Just $14.95*

5. On the Porch™ – *A Designer's Journal of Notes and Sketches.* 64 designs from Gold Seal™, Heartland Home Plans™ and Timeless Legacy™ – each one with a porch. Includes essays on the porch and its role in traditional design.

Book #7196P   *Only $2.95*

6. Photographed Portraits of an American Home™. 100 of our finest designs, beautifully photographed and tastefully presented among nostalgic photo album memories of "home". A must for any sales center's coffee-table.

Book #1017P   *Only $14.95*

7. Easy Living One-Story Designs™. 155 one-story home designs from the Gold Seal™, Heartland Home Plans™ and Timeless Legacy™ collections, together in one plan book.

Book #7096P   *Just $7.95*

Please include $2.95 Shipping & Handling when ordering one plan book, or $4.95 when ordering 2 or more plan books.

design basics inc.
HOME PLAN DESIGN SERVICE
11112 John Galt Blvd. Omaha, NE 68137-2384

$\mathcal{H}$elpful Tools you shouldn't build your new home without.

For many home buyers, visualizing the finished home is a challenge. Our **Study Print & Furniture Layout Guide** makes it easy. First, the Study Print provides views of all exterior elevations. Secondly, the Furniture Layout Guide provides you a "feel" for room sizes, with a 1/4 – scale floor plan, over 100 reusable furniture pieces and helpful tips on space planning. Available for any Design Basics plan. Please see order form at right.

Only $29.95

Our **Materials and Estimator's Workbook** is much more than just a materials list. The Workbook is designed to save valuable time in the budgeting process, ensure accurate and comparable bids and help eliminate errors. Prepared specifically for each Design Basics plan, it also allows you to track projected costs vs. actual expenditures throughout the construction process. Please see order form at right.

Only $50

$\mathcal{O}$RDERING
INFORMATION

✔	HOME PLAN PRODUCTS	PLAN NO.	QTY.	PRICE	SHIPPING & HANDLING	TOTAL
☐	1 Complete Set of Master Reproducible/Modifiable Vellum Prints				No Charge	$
☐	Add'l. Sets of Blueprints - $10.00 Except plan #9147, #9114 & #9119 - $35.00				$4.95 or No Charge if Shipped with plan	$
☐	Add'l. Sets of Mirror Reverse Blueprints - $10.00 Except Plan #9147, #9114 & #9119 - $35.00				$4.95 or No Charge if Shipped with plan	$
☐	Materials & Estimator's Workbook - $50.00 (Not Available for plans #9147, #9114 & #9119)				$4.95 or No Charge if Shipped with plan	$
☐	Study Print & Furniture Layout Guide–$29.95 *Study print (only) for plan #9147, #9114 & #9119 - $25				$4.95	$
☐	Photographed Portraits of an American Home™ – $14.95				$2.95	$
☐	Get it all for $97.00 Includes entire library of 11 Home Plan Books				$4.95	$
BOOK NUMBER		BOOK NAME			Individual Plan Books $2.95	$
					2 or More Plan Books $4.95	$

• All orders payable in U.S. funds only. • Shipping prices for Continental U.S. only • No refunds or exchanges, please.
• All Design Basics plans come with a basement foundation. • Alternate foundations available through our Custom Change Dept.

ORDER DIRECT: 800-947-7526
Monday – Friday: 7:00 a.m. – 6:00 p.m. CST
Fax your order any time: (402) 331-5507
Or mail to **Design Basics Inc.,**
11112 John Galt Blvd. • Omaha, NE 68137-2384

	Subtotal $
TX Res. Add 6.25% Tax (on plan #9147, #9114 & #9119 only) NE Residents Add 6.5% Sales Tax	$
	Total $

12	13	14						21	22	23
$455	$465							$545	$555	$565

24	25						34	36	38
$575	$585					$665	$675	$695	$715

39	CD36
$725	$760

CALL FOR CURRENT PRICING 1-800-947-7526

All prices include 1 set of Master Vellums

– Prices subject to change –

Company Name _____

Name _____

Address _____
<small>Packages cannot be shipped to a P.O. Box</small>

City _____ State _____ Zip _____

Above address is ☐ Business address   ☐ Residence address

Phone ( ) _____   Date _____

☐ VISA   ☐ AMEX
☐ MC   ☐ Discover
☐ Check or Money Order Enclosed

All COD's must be paid by Certified Check, Cashier's Check or Money Order.
(Additional $5.00 charge on COD Orders)

Exp.Date _____

Signature _____